## A full-color guide to 52 crystals and practices to elevate your everyday life

Are you looking to create your own luck? Or is today the day for breaking through blocks? Do you need to let go of what no longer serves you? Or do you simply want to sleep well, even if just for a night?

No matter who you are, crystals can provide a boost of energy and purpose, as well as serve as a tactile physical element to help you transform your everyday life. In this essential, full-color guide, you will discover 52 crystals that can help you 365 days of the year.

Co-author of *Crystal Muse* and founder of Energy Muse, Heather Askinosie, provides an abundance of key information, including each crystal's history and lore, origin, and intention, as well as simple three- to six-step practices for easy activation. She also shares a wealth of crystal combinations for intentions such as love, wealth, creativity, and happiness.

Whether you are an avid crystal fan or are a newbie, *CRYSTAL365* will help you to create a personalized action plan for your own style and goals for positive change.

# praise for CRYSTAL365

"I was always curious about crystals but had no idea where to start. The clear directions in CRYSTAL365 make using crystals simple and approachable. It showed me that doing something small, even for just a few minutes, can have a positive impact on my day."

— **Jenny McCarthy**, host of The Jenny McCarthy Show on SiriusXM and
New York Times best-selling author of Belly Laughs, Baby Laughs, and Louder Than Words

"CRYSTAL365 is chock-full of wisdom, magic, and practical
ideas to uplift and change your life. I love it!"

— **Christiane Northrup, M.D.**, New York Times best-selling author of Goddesses Never Age,
The Wisdom of Menopause, and Women's Bodies, Women's Wisdom

"Heather is not only a respected crystal expert, but she also brings in a kind
of palpable mystical and wildly generous relationship with whatever crystal she touches.
I've learned so much from her, and I call her the 'crystal whisperer.' I am so thrilled to
recommend this book. If you love crystals this book is for you!"

— **Colette Baron-Reid**, best-selling author of Uncharted and The Crystal Spirits Oracle

"The practices I've learned from CRYSTAL365 have given me new tools
to help me get more present and bring more attention to what I want to focus
on and move through. It's a beautiful way to take action, intention,
and ownership over supporting yourself and your vision."

— **Lori Harder**, best-selling author of A Tribe Called Bliss, podcast host, and entrepreneur

"CRYSTAL365 is a uniquely wonderful, modern-day guide to help anyone new
or experienced use the energy of crystals in their regular practice.
I'll be using this book in my daily meditation!"

— **Karena Dawn**, New York Times best-selling co-author of
Tone It Up: Balanced and Beautiful and co-founder of Tone It Up

"Add a little more color, mindfulness, and self-love to your heart by
opening this life-force-energy-filled book, CRYSTAL365."

— **Candice Kumai**, journalist, best-selling author of
Kintsugi Wellness, and host of the Wabi Sabi podcast

"I discovered Heather Askinosie's book Crystal Muse a few years ago and
so began my crystal obsession. CRYSTAL365 is the perfect book to deepen crystal
understanding and start the process of manifesting goals and dreams."

— **Christina Anstead**, mom, producer, and co-host of the Flip or Flop TV series

"CRYSTAL365 is the most practical guide to one of the most mysterious elements on
Earth—crystals. By sharing every possible day-to-day application of crystals to your life,
Heather has managed to bypass the new age, woo-woo approach to the topic."

— **Luke Storey**, motivational speaker and host of The Life Stylist podcast

"Heather is my crystal expert go-to! She has such a wonderful way of
making all the information super attainable and approachable, which makes it
easy to understand and apply it to my life. CRYSTAL365 is my newest obsession
and has given me the tools to manifest my dream life!"

— **Krista Williams**, co-founder of Almost 30, a top-ranked podcast and media company

HEATHER ASKINOSIE

# CRYSTAL365

crystals for everyday life

HAY HOUSE, INC.
Carlsbad, California • New York City
London • Sydney • New Delhi

For all the crystal lovers, soul seekers,
trailblazers, visionaries, light workers,
Earth keepers, and spiritually curious.

This one's for you.

Published in the United States by: Hay House, Inc.: www.hayhouse.com® • Published in Australia by: Hay House Australia Pty. Ltd.: www.hayhouse.com.au • Published in the United Kingdom by: Hay House UK, Ltd.: www.hayhouse.co.uk • Published in India by: Hay House Publishers India: www.hayhouse.co.in

Indexer: Carol Roberts
Cover and interior design: Karla Baker
Interior photos/illustrations: Energy Muse

Library of Congress Cataloging-in-Publication Data
Names: Askinosie, Heather, author.
Title: Crystal365 : crystals for everyday life and your guide to health, wealth, and balance / Heather Askinosie.
Other titles: Crystal 365
Description: 1st edition. | Carlsbad, California : Hay House, Inc., 2019. |
Summary: "Transform and energize your everyday life with this essential guide for 52 crystals to be used 365 days of the year. Co-author of Crystal Muse and co-founder of Energy Muse, Heather Askinosie, provides an abundance of key information, including each crystal's history and lore, origin, and intention, as well as a simple three- to six-step action plan for easy activation. Also included are crystal combinations for intentions such as love, wealth, creativity, happiness, and more.
Whether you are an avid crystal fan or just appreciate crystals' aesthetic beauty, Crystal365 will help you to incorporate crystals into your daily life in a more meaningful and conscious way with action plans that can be personalized to your own style and goals for transformation"-- Provided by publisher.
Identifiers: LCCN 2019021579 | ISBN 9781401958268 (hardcover) | ISBN 9781401958275 (e-book)
Subjects: LCSH: Crystals--Miscellanea.
Classification: LCC BF1442.C78 A85 2019 | DDC 133/.2548--dc23
LC record available at https://lccn.loc.gov/2019021579

Hardcover ISBN: 978-1-4019-5826-8
e-book ISBN: 978-1-4019-5827-5
e-audio ISBN: 978-14019-5828-2

10  9  8  7  6  5  4  3  2  1
1st edition, November 2019
Printed in the United States of America

# 3

# 30 CRYSTAL COMBINATIONS
221

# author's note

Crystals have transformed my life. As a seeker of truth, I've tried
many different forms of self-help techniques. Some have stuck;
some have not. For the past 30 years, crystals have been the
one constant tool that has always worked for me.

Crystals have helped me to create positive growth in my relationships, family,
career, and so much more. I went from feeling like something was missing to
being completely in tune with my life's calling, all due to my connection with
crystals—and it's not just me! Crystals have improved the lives of my family,
my friends, and people all over the world. I get the privilege of seeing it every
day, as someone lucky enough to be in this industry.

   The crystal formulas and combinations in this book are the result of de-
cades of practice. I'm sharing these easy ways to get results because I want
you to get straight to the healing, without feeling confused or hesitant.

   Working with crystals doesn't have to be complicated. When my business partner, Timmi, and I founded our crystal company, Energy Muse,
nearly 20 years ago, I had been studying and researching ways to work
with crystals for years. In all that time, I came to realize that all it takes
is the simple act of connecting with a crystal to enhance your intention,
which then changes your life.

   By combining a daily intention with a crystal practice, you can achieve
major results. Crystals hold the wisdom and transformative energy of
the Earth. Connecting with a crystal will deepen the bond you have with
yourself and your natural state of being. You'll feel grounded in who you
are and get clear on what you want. It is from this state that you can make
choices and take actions toward living your truest, fullest life.

Heather Askinosie

# WHAT CAN CRYSTALS
# DO FOR YOU?

Has life ever gotten in the way of you achieving your personal goals and dreams? It's easy to get distracted or stalled. Responsibilities can take precedence over dreams, and your goals can get pushed so far to the side that you give up on them completely.
It doesn't have to be this way.

Now is the time to start living your best life.

Crystals hold a transformational energy that can help you change your life. As Albert Einstein is reported to have said, everything in life is vibration. Healing crystals carry powerful vibrations that connect you with the power of Mother Earth, and they provide a physical, tangible way for you to feel, connect with, and benefit from those vibrations. They help you to realign and recalibrate your own energy, helping you to reach a higher state of being.

Due to their structure, crystals emit energy at a constant frequency. When a crystal is placed on or near an area of your body emitting a lower frequency, the energy of your body rises to match the crystal's higher frequency. This attunement helps you to move past mental, physical, and spiritual blockages and reach a higher vibrational state where you can stay focused and positive. Similarly, when you pair a crystal with an intention or a personal goal, the crystal amplifies the energy of your intention. By amplifying your intention and aligning your energy with a higher vibration, crystals make pursuing your goals that much easier.

Whether you're looking to enhance an area of your life or let go of something holding you back, let crystals be the key to making it a reality. Crystals act as tools to ground you, center you, and empower you to create lasting change. They provide you with a physical representation of your intentions and goals, something you can touch, hold on to, and connect with on a daily basis. But it's important to remember, it's not the crystal making the change; you are making the change. It's not doing the work; you're doing the work. It's an ally on your journey. A tool to help you get where you want to go.

Whether you want to prioritize your health, increase your financial wealth, or cultivate love, crystals will help you bring your intentions to life. Using them in simple ways in your daily life allows you to stay focused, motivated, and excited to create the life you've always dreamed of.

## SINCE THE BEGINNING OF TIME . . .

Having witnessed the evolution of life for millions of years, crystals have stored the energy of transformation. Working with them is a powerful way to connect with that transformational energy—and almost every civilization since the beginning of time has learned to harness their energy.

Many ancient civilizations used crystals for protection in battle, during travel, and against evil forces. Ancient Greeks rubbed crushed Hematite on their bodies before going to battle to render them invincible. Ancient Roman sailors used Aquamarine to protect them at sea. The ancient Egyptians inlaid their coffins and lined the tombs of their most beloved pharaohs with crystals such as Lapis Lazuli and Carnelian to ward off evil and provide safe passage into the afterlife. One of the most well-known kings, King Tutankhamen, had an iconic mask with inlays of Lapis Lazuli around the eyes, Obsidian in the pupils, and Carnelian, Turquoise, and many other gemstones in the decorative collar.

Other civilizations used crystals for spiritual practices. In the Han dynasty, Chinese emperors were buried in elaborate Jade suits as a symbol of wealth and power. Some of these suits consisted of as many as 2,400 individual pieces that were carefully sewn together. Ancient Egyptians also used crystals in their burial rituals. They placed Clear Quartz over the foreheads of their dead as they believed that it would help guide them in their journey to the afterlife.

Furthermore, crystals were used to bring color and vibrancy to everyday life. By grinding up crystals into a powder, the ancient Egyptians were able to create a rainbow of cosmetics! They transformed crystals into pastes for eyeshadows and lipsticks. Always depicted with bold eye makeup, Queen Cleopatra's signature bright blue and green eyeshadow looks were made from Malachite and Lapis Lazuli powders.

The transformational powers of crystals have survived the test of time and remain just as relevant today. Although crystals have been around longer than humans have inhabited Earth, scientists are only just now beginning to understand their significance. The more that crystals are researched, the more prominent they become in our present-day lives.

# CRYSTALS ARE TECHNOLOGY

Your computer, television, phone, and other electronic devices probably have LCD screens, which stands for liquid-crystal display. These screens rely on liquid crystals to produce images. So you are likely already working with crystals every day!

Crystals are also prominent in other technological advances. Silicon, one of the primary elements in Quartz, is the basic material used in computer chips and solar panels. When you store your information on a computer chip, you are really using a form of Quartz crystal. Hitachi, a Japanese technology group, capitalized on the power of Quartz to hold information when they developed a "quartz glass" chip, which was projected to store data for 100 million years. Just as Quartz crystals have been able to survive even the most catastrophic events on Earth, so too will these Quartz storage technologies and the information within them.

The full power of crystals is only just beginning to be discovered, but it's clear that these stones are going to be even more widely used in the future. And just as crystals are an integral part of technology, they can also become an integral part of improving your own life.

# ONE CRYSTAL, ONE PURPOSE

Every goal begins with an intention. Intentions help you to focus on a specific aspect of your life and commit to creating a change. When creating intentions, the first step is to define what you want to transform. Once you are clear on what changes you want to make, you can work with a crystal to bring those changes to life. Follow this simple formula to get your desired results:

## INTENTION + CRYSTAL + PRACTICE = TRANSFORMATION

Combining a specific intention with a specific crystal and a specific practice is the perfect recipe for transformation. Your crystal holds your intention and reminds you to stay on track, while the customized practice gives you the direction and tangible steps to make it a reality. When used daily, this formula will help you bring your long-term goals to life. For short-term goals and quick transformations, this formula helps to bring focus to a specific outcome. This formula can be used over and over again, each time with a new intention, a new crystal, and a new action plan.

Because there are crystals for every intention, crystals can help you with every facet of your life. If you're looking for love, go for Rose Quartz. For wealth, call upon Pyrite. For health, work with Turquoise. And just as your intentions and the crystals

you use will differ, the ways in which you work with them will differ as well. Some intentions will take longer to work toward, like finding new love or creating wealth, while others will be more of a quick fix, such as shifting negativity. Still others will require everyday action, like focusing on health.

Even though anyone can work with crystals, it can be confusing to know where to begin and how to progress. This book aims to take out the guesswork by showing you how to use one crystal for one purpose with one practice. All you need to do is pick which one (or ones) you want to focus on, and use the best crystal we have pinpointed to match that intention. Then you use the customized formula to reach your specific goals so that you can get the most out of your crystal journey.

## HOW TO USE CRYSTAL365

The 52 crystals in this book can help you 365 days a year. These crystals have been carefully chosen as the most powerful and effective, yet simple, tools to help you in your everyday life.

While making your way through the 52 crystals to improve and progress your life, you may find that you need to work with some crystals longer than others. Certain areas of your life may require more time and focus. The time frame will be different for everyone and every intention, so it's important to customize how you use this book and your crystal practice to what works for you. You may choose to focus on one crystal/intention at a time, or you may find that you can balance several crystals/ intentions at once. Learn your own unique style of working with crystals and follow that, as long as you approach your intentions with the same level of commitment.

Additionally, this book includes crystal combinations for 30 intentions, including love, wealth, creativity, and happiness. When you work with a combination of crystals versus a singular crystal, you are able to heighten the energy of your intention by addressing the different layers and multifaceted nature of your goal. Use these crystal combinations to amplify your intention and supercharge your crystal practice.

Let CRYSTAL365 be your go-to crystal guide anytime you are looking to make a shift in your life—52 crystals, 52 intentions, 52 weeks, 365 days a year.

# CLEANSING YOUR CRYSTALS

Crystals work best when they are cleansed because, over time, crystals absorb and accumulate energy from the environment around them. To ensure that your crystal is clean and ready to use, here are four simple ways to cleanse your crystal.

The Sun burns off old energy and refills your crystal with vibrancy and light. The Full Moon is when the moon is at its brightest, and bathing your crystals under it restores them to their brightest form. Sound breaks up any stuck or stored energy and restores harmony. The smoke created when burning sage carries away any low vibrational energy stored in the crystal. You can use any of these methods:

## sun

Place your crystal outside in the light of
the Sun for four hours or more.

## full moon

Place your crystal outside under the light of the
Full Moon for four hours or more.

## sound

Download and play the music of Tibetan singing bowls,
the om mantra, or Beethoven's Fifth Symphony.

## sage

Immerse your crystal in the smoke of
burning sage for at least 30 seconds.

As a general guideline, it is recommended that you cleanse your crystal every time you set a new intention, or at least once every 30 days.

As you read through the 52 crystals and crystal combinations in this book, you'll find that some crystal practices recommend you cleanse your crystal as part of the practice. When a practice involves releasing heavy or dense energy, the crystal absorbs those lower vibrations as you release them from your mind, body, and spirit. In these cases, cleansing is a necessary part of the practice to maintain the vibrancy of your crystal.

When cleansing is not specified as part of a practice, you can rely on your own schedule for cleansing your crystal.

## THE MEANING OF NUMBERS

Every number has a different meaning and significance. As part of the crystal practices in this book, you will be instructed to repeat your intention a specific number of times. This will reprogram your energy to help you achieve your goal.

1 NEW BEGINNINGS: Saying something one time represents a fresh start.

2 HARMONY: Saying something two times represents peace and unity.

3 ACTION: Saying something three times represents taking action.

4 BALANCE: Saying something four times brings stability.

5 CHANGE: Saying something five times represents transformation.

6 LOVE: Saying something six times represents love.

7 HEALING: Saying something seven times has a therapeutic effect.

8 WEALTH: Saying something eight times attracts money, prosperity, and abundance.

9 COMPLETION: Saying something nine times represents the end of a cycle.

# 52 CRYSTALS

To get started, simply identify an area of your life that you want to transform, and look up the crystal to match. Each of the 52 crystals in this section is paired with an intention and a practice to help you bring your desired outcome to life. Working with crystals has never been so easy! Because of the range of intentions and crystals included in this section, you'll soon find yourself reaching for one (or more) of these 52 crystals every single day of every week in the year.

# agate

balancing your life

WHEN TO USE IT

When you are spreading yourself too thin

ORIGIN

Found in Africa, Brazil, India, Morocco,
the United States, and many other places

COLOR

Clear, milky white, gray, blue, green, pink, brown,
or multicolored; often banded

## HISTORY & LORE

Agate has been found among artifacts of the Stone Age man in France dating back to 20,000 and 16,000 B.C. Some Agate found in Australia, however, can date back 2.72 to 3.50 billion years.

For the past 6,000 years, Agate has been used by various civilizations. In ancient Mesopotamia, Agate signified strength and was carved into cylinder seals utilized for official documents in business transactions. Because of Agate's strength, many of these seals have survived unharmed and continue to give historians a deeper understanding of that era.

In ancient China, wearing Agate was believed to purify the mind and energize a person's chi. During medieval times, Agate was tied to the horns of oxen to promote a good harvest. In some legends, Agate is believed to calm thunder and lightning storms.

## WHAT CAN AGATE DO FOR YOU?

Agate creates balance in your life. If you're like most people, you're probably juggling family, work, health, relationships, and more. In an effort to show up for each of these endeavors, it can be easy to overlook the importance of distributing your energy in a healthy way.

Like walking a tightrope, prioritizing how you distribute your energy is essential to finding equilibrium in your life. Learning to better manage your time and energy helps you to accomplish your goals and get you to where you need to go. Think of Agate as being the pole you need to stay balanced while walking your tightrope. Agate keeps you constantly assessing where to best focus your time. Creating this balance isn't crucial just for optimal health, happiness, and well-being, but also for being successful in all that you do.

Agate encourages you to pinpoint the areas in your life that are taking up too much time and energy and put them into perspective. Achieving your goals while also living up to your responsibilities requires careful consideration. The first step is to find a balance between what you *want* and what you *need*. Agate helps you come into alignment with what you truly need on a deeper level. After reevaluating what's important to you—whether it's family, love, health, work, or a personal passion—Agate reminds you to reconsider devoting energy to the less important things.

When your energy feels pulled in multiple directions, try working with Agate to get centered on what's most valuable to you. Start by assessing your life as it is now so you can identify the areas that need rearranging. Once you recognize the areas that are out of balance, Agate helps you decide where to direct more or less of your energy, and then encourages you to come up with a plan to bring your life back into balance.

# I balance all areas of my life.

◇

1  On a piece of paper, draw a circle and divide it into 8 equal parts.

2  Fill in each section with one of your top 8 values (e.g., family, career, health, etc.).

3  Rank your values from 1 to 8, 1 being the most out of balance.

4  Hold your Agate in your hand and say out loud,

"I balance _____."
*(Fill in what you labeled as value 1 in step 3.)*
Repeat 2 more times.

5  Place your crystal on the related area of the circle. Focus on this area of your life. Ask yourself: *How could I bring more balance into this area?*

6  Once you've created more balance in this area, move your Agate to the next area you want to focus on and repeat step 5.

7  Continue steps 5 and 6 until you've brought more balance to all 8 of your values.

# amazonite

being hopeful

WHEN TO USE IT

When you feel pessimistic or have lost hope

ORIGIN

Found in Brazil, Canada, India, Madagascar,
Mozambique, the United States, and many other places

COLOR

Bright hues of blue and green

## HISTORY & LORE

Even though Amazonite is named after the Amazon River due to its rich, watery hues, it is actually not found near the Amazon. The closest Amazonite can be found to its namesake is in Minas Gerais, Brazil. Still, this stone has a long-standing connection with local inhabitants of the Amazon region. Linked to female warriors, Amazonite is said to have adorned the shields of Amazonian tribal women warriors hailing from roughly the 10th century B.C.

The bright green to bluish-green stone was also a favorite among the ancient Egyptians. The gold death mask found in King Tutankhamen's tomb was adorned with Amazonite inlays. Referred to as the "Stone of Hope," Amazonite has long been revered for attracting hope and faith to those who wear it.

## WHAT CAN AMAZONITE DO FOR YOU?

Amazonite gives you hope. A pessimistic attitude prevents you from living the life you want. Amazonite inspires a hopeful, empowering mind-set so you can move forward with optimism. Working with this crystal will train your mind to expect positive outcomes. With this heightened sense of optimism, Amazonite pulls you out of the darkness so you can stand in the light.

Amazonite's energy connects to your heart and brings joy, love, and optimism. It helps you replace low vibrational energy in your heart with hope and a glass-half-full perspective. This crystal clears away your fears, doubts, and worries and encourages you to believe that something good will come out of all your efforts. The hope that this crystal instills is a powerful way to motivate yourself to keep striving, no matter what you are going through. Amazonite is your constant reminder to have hope that it will all work out in the end.

When you have lost hope, turn to your Amazonite crystal for a boost of hopefulness and confidence. Have you been experiencing relationship difficulty in your dating life? Are you feeling discouraged about how your job hunt is going? Are there other areas of your life that have you feeling disappointed and disheartened? Amazonite gives you the hope you need to persevere and keep pursuing your goals, despite the setbacks, obstacles, and perceived limitations. This crystal refuses to let you give up on your desires or get stuck in a state of despair. Instead, it helps you keep your hope alive by believing in a brighter tomorrow and an even brighter day after that. It reminds you that good things are waiting for you just around the corner. With a little hope, Amazonite empowers and motivates you to stay strong in the face of adversity. Let it encourage you to be hopeful in all of your endeavors.

# I am hopeful.

1 Hold your Amazonite in your dominant hand and say out loud, "I am hopeful," 3 times.

2 Close your eyes and bring to mind a current situation in your life that is leaving you less than hopeful.

3 Squeeze your Amazonite and ask yourself, *What is this situation trying to show me, teach me, or do for me?*

4 Visualize the healing blue-green color of the crystal washing over you. Feel the energy of this crystal lifting your spirit and filling it with hope.

# amethyst

## finding peace of mind

WHEN TO USE IT

When you want to feel peaceful and relaxed

ORIGIN

Found in Brazil, Canada, India, Madagascar, Namibia,
Russia, the United States, Uruguay, and Zambia

COLOR

Ranges from light lavender to deep violet

## HISTORY & LORE

Amethyst, due to its deep purple color, is associated with Bacchus, the Greek god of wine. Large drinking vessels used for water and wine were often carved from this stone. Roman matrons believed that wearing Amethyst would help to guarantee fidelity. Cleopatra is said to have worn a signet ring made of Amethyst to represent enlightenment and love.

Amethyst is one of the 12 gemstones that lined the walls of heaven in Revelation. In the Roman Catholic Church, the pure color of Amethyst is associated with the wine transfigured to Christ's blood in the sacrament of Mass. Amethyst has been a signature gemstone for bishops and is often incorporated into their ceremonial rings.

## WHAT AMETHYST CAN DO FOR YOU?

Amethyst brings you peace of mind. At the end of an exhausting day or in the middle of a chaotic meeting, have you ever wished for even just a minute of peace and quiet? These moments of total stillness and calm may be infrequent, but you can access peace even in less idyllic moments. Amethyst helps you find inner peace, regardless of the noise around you. Use Amethyst as your reminder that peace is within you. Its high vibrational purple color guides you to turn inward so you can get back to a state of equilibrium. On a deep soul level, your spirit knows that you have everything you need to find inner peace.

With its relaxing and calming energies, Amethyst helps to ease away any disturbances, distractions, or anything else taking up space in your mind. Through working with this crystal, you will be able to create a bit more space between your thoughts. Acting as a natural stress reliever, Amethyst purifies your mind of worry, anxiety, and all other day-to-day stresses so you can settle into a more tranquil and peaceful state of mind. It emits a spa-like energy of relaxation, which works to soothe your mind, body, and spirit.

Simply by working with Amethyst, you can bring about peaceful energy—wherever and whenever. Are cars honking all around you on the freeway? Are your kids screaming? Is your email inbox overflowing? Even in a frenzied, fast-paced world, Amethyst is the touchstone that reconnects you to calmness. This crystal will encourage you to replace the external noise with internal peace and quiet. Rather than waiting for the world to get quiet, turn inward and give yourself the peace you are searching for. Amethyst will help you to tune in to your inner peace right now, and anytime.

# I am at peace.

1   Before you go to bed, hold your Amethyst over your third eye (on the center of your forehead, slightly above your brows).

2   Close your eyes and take 7 deep breaths. Visualize Amethyst's purple color filling your mind and calming your thoughts.

3   Say to yourself internally, *I am at peace*, 7 times.

4   Place your Amethyst on your nightstand. Continue to breathe deeply as you slowly drift off to sleep.

# angel aura quartz

making time to play

WHEN TO USE IT

When you've lost touch with the fun side of life

ORIGIN

On virtually every continent

COLOR

White with a reflective rainbow sheen

24

## HISTORY & LORE

Angel Aura Quartz is created through a process called electroplating. Electroplating transforms Clear Quartz crystals into colorfully flashy stones with a milky, opaque surface and full spectrum of iridescent hues. This treatment uses precious metals like platinum and silver.

This rainbow-flashing crystal has risen in popularity since the 1980s and has quickly become a renowned healing tool within the crystal world. Although crystal healers traditionally favor natural crystals, Angel Aura Quartz seems to be the exception that breaks this "rule." Many believe that the combination of the high-quality metal with natural Quartz crystal amplifies the energy of its original state.

## WHAT CAN ANGEL AURA QUARTZ DO FOR YOU?

Angel Aura Quartz urges you to have more fun. As a kid, playtime is built into your schedule and is one of the activities you most look forward to in the day. It offers the opportunity to be creative, express yourself, and take risks without worldly consequences. But somewhere between youth and adulthood, the idea of play becomes less important. As you get older and your life gets busier, you no longer prioritize playing. And as a result, you don't do enough of it.

This rainbow crystal reminds you that making the time to play is equally important for adults. The biggest benefit to play is the alleviation of stress. When you play, your body releases mood-elevating endorphins that boost your sense of well-being. At the same time, playing is a simple way to remove stress from the body and replace it with feel-good emotions like joy and happiness.

Angel Aura Quartz helps you to embrace your playful side. It sparkles with the colors of the rainbow and reminds you to seek out the whimsy in life. This crystal's jovial energy makes it the perfect antidote when you're taking life too seriously. Instead of getting stuck in the stress and chaos of everyday life, this crystal gives you permission to prioritize fun! While there are plenty of things in life that you should take seriously, Angel Aura Quartz helps you to lighten up so you can be present for the things that make you smile and laugh. You deserve to have fun!

When your favorite song comes on the radio, turn up the volume and sing your heart out! Dance like nobody's watching! This crystal wants you to remember that you're really just a big kid. Allowing yourself to play helps you to get back in touch with your inner happiness so you can be the best version of yourself for the people and obligations in your life.

If you can't bring to mind the last time you cried from laughing, Angel Aura Quartz is the crystal for you.

# Go play!

1   Hold your Angel Aura Quartz in your hand and say out loud, "Go play!"

2   Plan something fun to do within the next 48 hours. It doesn't have to be long, but use this time to play, laugh, and let loose.

3   Take your Angel Aura Quartz with you whenever it's time to play.

# angelite

connecting with angels

WHEN TO USE IT

When you feel alone

ORIGIN

Found in India, Peru, and many other places

COLOR

Light blue

## HISTORY & LORE

Angelite is a relatively new crystal, discovered in Peru in 1987. It is also sometimes referred to as Blue Anhydrite. This name comes from the Greek word *anhydras*, meaning "without water." That is a reference to the stone's unique physical property, as a dehydrated gypsum. Angelite only develops in areas where gypsum crystals once had contact with water. Over millions of years, the water evaporates and the gypsum crystals get compressed, resulting in the formation of Angelite.

The name Angelite comes from its ethereal light blue color and the belief that this crystal can enhance one's connection with angels or the divine realm.

## WHAT CAN ANGELITE DO FOR YOU?

Angelite is a peaceful crystal that embodies the gentle vibrations of your guardian angels. Working with this crystal infuses your spirit with serenity and positivity. It will heighten your awareness of the invisible world and remind you that angels are all around you. Even just gazing at its heavenly blue hues invokes a connection with the celestial realm. When you feel its divine energies of support, Angelite acts as a direct line between you and the angel realm.

The tranquility of this crystal will quiet the spirit so you can surrender to a more vulnerable state. This sense of openness and humility allows you to ask your angels for the help you need and to be receptive to the answers. Did you detect an underlying signal in the song that's playing on the radio? Did you have a conversation with someone who inadvertently gave you the perfect advice on a situation you've been struggling with? Did you experience a sudden scent in the air that reminded you of someone you were just thinking about? Angels send messages in many different ways and often when you least expect them. Angelite helps you to recognize these subtle messages from your angels.

When you tune in to Angelite's frequency, you feel your angels' divine love and remember that you are not alone. Even in your darkest hour, you can call on Angelite for support. With its soothing and nurturing blue color and energy, this crystal reminds you that there is always someone to reach out to—in both the physical and invisible worlds. It connects you to your support system. Reminiscent of an angel's wings, Angelite helps open up your lung space to unite you back with your breath. By connecting with your breath, Angelite invites you to find within the feelings of love and support that you are looking for outside of yourself. Angelite helps you come home to yourself and feel the presence of your angels, so you will never feel alone again.

# Surround me with angels.

1 Before you go to bed, hold your Angelite in your hand and say out loud: "Angels, please surround me. I ask for help with

_____

*[state your request]*
and that you make your presence known in a dream or by giving me a clear sign tomorrow. This way I will know you surround me. Thank you, thank you, thank you."

2 Place your Angelite under your pillow while you sleep.

3 Carry your Angelite in your pocket or purse throughout the day and ask your angels to surround you.

# apatite

*finding inspiration*

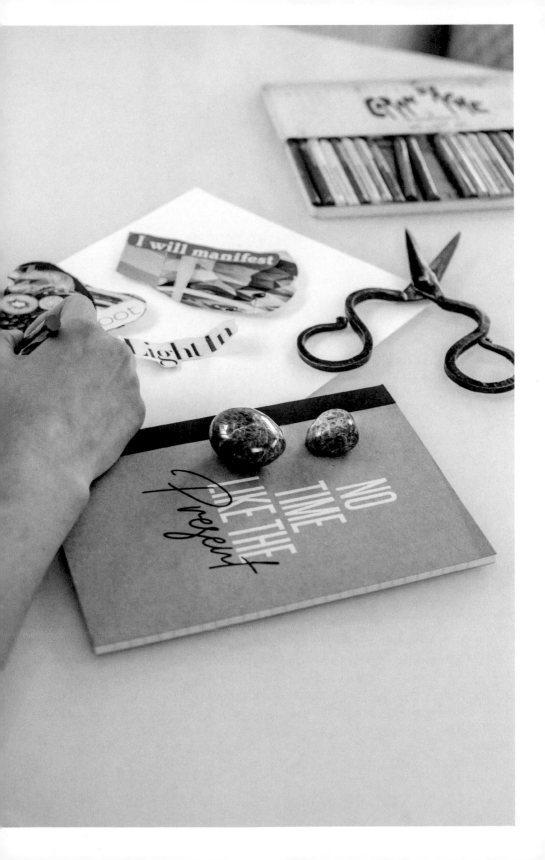

## HISTORY & LORE

Apatite gets its name from the Greek word for "deceit." This name does not come from any character flaw of the stone, but because Apatite is so often mistaken for other crystals like Beryl, Amethyst, and Peridot. In fact, Apatite is still a source of difficulty for mineralogists trying to identify the stone. *Apatite* is an umbrella term used to describe many varieties of the stone that have similar but differing chemical compositions, including fluorapatite, hydroxylapatite, and chlorapatite.

Apatite is composed of a mineral called calcium phosphate. If that sounds familiar to you, it is likely because it is the same mineral found in bones and teeth. That's why consuming calcium is recommended in order to have strong, healthy bones! That's also why it is believed that connecting with Apatite's energy can enhance your physical health.

## WHAT CAN APATITE DO FOR YOU?

Apatite will help you find inspiration. Being inspired is like having sparks go off in your mind that not only get you excited about an idea, but also hand you the tools to bring it to life. When you work with Apatite, you never have to wait another day to pursue whatever it is in life that calls to you.

Apatite reinvigorates your appetite for life—that internal force that keeps you hungry for new ideas, projects, and experiences. It helps you to see the opportunities that surround you, and invites you to pursue them. Connecting with Apatite awakens the bright-eyed version of yourself. This crystal wants you to deep dive into your interests and go beyond the surface. Apatite is a future-oriented crystal. Working with it fuels the ambitious and passionate version of yourself that is not only exhilarated, but also committed to taking action. It helps you seek out inspiration so that you do more than *feel* excited; you can actually *do* what excites you.

One of the best crystals for entrepreneurs or anyone looking to take up a new project or idea, Apatite's blue color reminds you to stay fluid, be open, and tune in to the possibility of getting inspired in different ways and places. No matter how big or small your project may be, think of Apatite as your brainstorming buddy, helping you draw inspiration from different places and bring them all together to help you get going on your ideas. Are you starting a new business? Learning a new skill? Cooking? Use this crystal to stir up the excitement, enthusiasm, and motivation you have within so that you can get started on your passion project.

# I am inspired!

1   Hold your Apatite in your hand and say out loud, "I am inspired!"

2   Create a vision board by collecting inspirational quotes and photos from magazines or downloading them from your computer. Get a sturdy material, such as wood or poster board, and glue your images to it. Decorate your board with anything that makes you feel inspired and motivated.

3   Place your vision board in your living room, bedroom, or work space— somewhere you will see it often.

4   Place your Apatite on top of your vision board for 7 days to soak up your inspiration.

5   After the 7 days, carry your Apatite with you in your pocket or purse whenever you need a spark of inspiration.

# apophyllite

staying positive

## HISTORY & LORE

Discovered in the early 1800s, Apophyllite's name was inspired by the Greek words *apo*, meaning "away from," and *phylliso*, meaning "to leaf." It is named for the soft crystal's tendency to flake off when heated. This crystal occurs in many different shapes and colors, often developing into exceptionally large specimens.

For a period of time, the differing varieties of Apophyllite were classified into two subcategories: Fluorapophyllite and Hydroxyapophyllite. This was based on the ratio of minerals within the stone. Today, however, they are all once again simply referred to as Apophyllite.

Legend suggests that Apophyllite was used to help those who participated in fire walking. Participants would hold Apophyllite in their hands to reach a highly meditative state, and then use the stone to help cool their feet.

## WHAT CAN APOPHYLLITE DO FOR YOU?

Apophyllite encourages you to be more positive. Staying positive is a skill that can be developed with training and perseverance. It's also a choice that we make many times throughout the day. Choosing to stay positive isn't always easy. Have you ever noticed yourself reverting to negativity, even when your life is going well? Perhaps that's because negativity has become your default state of mind. Instead of focusing on all the things you *don't* have in your life, Apophyllite reminds you to focus on all the things you actually *do*.

Apophyllite's high vibrational energy purifies your mind and lifts your spirits. The twinkling shimmer of this white crystal offers you a moment to breathe a little deeper and bathe in its radiant positivity. Apophyllite encourages you to have a positive attitude, not just a positive thought. It trains you to make the most out of the situation and go into even the most daunting situations with your head held high. With the positive outlook that Apophyllite provides, not even the toughest times can get you down. This crystal will help you turn failures into lessons and end the habit of saying "Yes, *but* . . ."

Being positive does not mean you are ignoring your misfortunes. In fact, the power of positive thinking inspires you to find a constructive way to respond to them. By concentrating on the lesson or opportunity within every situation, Apophyllite gives you positivity when you need it most.

# I choose to be positive today.

◇

1   In the morning, hold your Apophyllite in your hands and say out loud, "I choose to be positive today," 3 times.

2   Place your Apophyllite in an area where you will see it every day as a visual reminder to maintain a positive mind-set.

3   Throughout your day, when you find yourself approaching a negative mind-set, consciously catch yourself, pause, and reflect on how you can shift your thought from the negative to the positive.

# aquamarine

accepting yourself

**WHEN TO USE IT**

When you need to embrace all aspects of who you are

**ORIGIN**

Found in Brazil, India, Mexico, Russia,
the United States, and many other places

**COLOR**

Light blue and transparent

## HISTORY & LORE

The name *Aquamarine* comes from the Latin words *aqua*, meaning "water," and *marina*, meaning "of the sea." Aquamarine is believed to be a lucky talisman, protecting sailors from rough waters as well as seasickness. This theme of protection is consistent in all of Aquamarine's lore.

According to Greek legend, Aquamarine was first considered to be a stone of the Sirens. Sailors and fishermen used it to protect themselves against the perilous "Siren call." In Roman tradition, Aquamarine was considered to be the gemstone of Neptune, god of the sea. A Roman man would present his bride with Aquamarine as a wedding gift to invoke love. Today, it is considered the appropriate stone to give to a spouse on the 19th wedding anniversary, as it is said to rekindle lost marital love.

## WHAT CAN AQUAMARINE DO FOR YOU?

Aquamarine helps you to fully accept who you are. Giving yourself permission to honor all the different parts of you—the parts you love, and even the parts you don't—is one of the most empowering things you can do for yourself. When you feel yourself leaning toward self-judgment, Aquamarine reminds you to open your heart and treat yourself with kindness. Its energy, like its color, is gentle and soothing. If you tend to be hard on yourself, Aquamarine teaches you how to go easier so you can be more loving and compassionate with yourself.

One of the first steps on the journey toward self-acceptance is to bring awareness to those thoughts and behaviors that come between you and your ability to accept yourself. Aquamarine brings light to the ways in which you judge, mistreat, or criticize yourself. Its tranquil, calming energy helps to wash away the critical thoughts and inner commentary that prevent you from accepting yourself wholeheartedly.

Work with Aquamarine to eliminate thoughts that threaten your self-acceptance and replace them with ones that affirm who you are. Instead of putting yourself down, it encourages you to lift yourself up. Own who you are. Be at home with yourself. Embrace your unique and beautiful qualities. Let Aquamarine give you the greatest gift you can give yourself: *accepting who you are.*

Because Aquamarine holds the fluid energy of water, it encourages you to embrace its nature and remain fluid with yourself. You are ever changing, which means you must continually accept who you are in every stage of your life. Who you are today might not be the same as who you will be tomorrow. Use the fluidity and flexibility of this stone to give yourself the space and permission to evolve, and to embrace yourself during the highs and the lows. Aquamarine encourages you to accept yourself fully today, tomorrow, and every day of your life.

# I accept who I am today and every day.

◇

1  Hold your Aquamarine in your non-writing hand.

2  While holding your Aquamarine, write down any self-critical thoughts that keep you from fully accepting yourself. Be honest and let your feelings come out on paper.

3  Without reading what you wrote, rip your paper into tiny pieces and throw it away.

4  Hold your Aquamarine over your heart and visualize the energy of Aquamarine washing away all of your self-criticism and filling that space up with self-acceptance.

5  As you hold your Aquamarine over you heart, say out loud, "I accept who I am today and every day," 6 times.

6  Carry Aquamarine in your bra, pocket, or purse throughout the day as a gentle reminder to accept yourself.

# aragonite

### releasing anger

WHEN TO USE IT

When you're ready to let go of anger

ORIGIN

Found in Austria, Greece, Italy, Mexico, Morocco,
Namibia, Spain, and the United States

COLOR

Burnt amber to rust

## HISTORY & LORE

Aragonite gets its name from the region of Spain known as Molina de Aragon. It forms around hot mineral springs and develops into a wide range of shapes, from columns to prisms.

In Greek mythology, Aragonite was attuned to Gaia, the Mother Earth goddess. It was believed to be an Earth healer, able to transform stress and clear blockages.

In Japanese mythology, Aragonite is closely associated with Amaterasu, the goddess of the Sun. Amaterasu's brother, the storm god, became angry and forced cruelty upon the Earth and heavens. Amaterasu realized that her inner light was the best antidote for her brother's darkness. Aragonite, believed to free you from the path of darkness, became known as the stone that helps to remedy anger.

## WHAT CAN ARAGONITE DO FOR YOU?

Aragonite helps you to release your anger. Instead of bottling up your anger—even if you feel it is justified—use Aragonite to learn how to manage and let go of anger for the sake of your own sanity.

Let Aragonite serve as a visual representation of what anger looks like. It encourages you to look at your sharper edges, just like those on this crystal. It helps you become aware of your triggers and directs you to come up with a game plan to handle anger when it bubbles up to the surface. Aragonite's amber-colored columns expand outward in all directions, just like anger does when it explodes. Even though this crystal acts as a visual representation of the explosion of anger that is possible, it also contains a network of pathways pointing in different directions. Use these paths as a symbol of your ability to choose how you respond to anger when it arises within you.

Aragonite is a stone of conscious awareness. It pushes you to be proactive and address your anger before it takes a toll on you. Use Aragonite as an anger check on your emotions. Rather than holding in pent-up anger or allowing your anger to explode, Aragonite reminds you to stop and reflect. Once you've had time to process and evaluate how you feel and why, Aragonite helps you to temper your anger. With a cooler disposition and clearer head, you will be able to peacefully and calmly release your anger and move on to a healthier mentality.

If you have already experienced an outburst of anger, this crystal offers you the choice to shift your behavior. It teaches you to regain control of your emotions and come back to your mental game plan for managing anger. Rather than justifying or blaming, can you take a look at yourself and shift your reaction? Working with Aragonite won't change the situation, but it can shift how you respond to triggers and outbursts of anger toward a more positive approach.

# My anger no longer controls me.

1  When you feel your anger rising, squeeze your Aragonite in your hand and close your eyes.

2  Visualize your anger being absorbed by the crystal.

3  In your head, say, *My anger no longer controls me,* 9 times.

4  Continue to hold on to your Aragonite until your anger dissipates.

5  Place your Aragonite in the Sun for 4 hours to cleanse the anger it absorbed.

# aventurine

creating your own luck

## HISTORY & LORE

Aventurine comes from the Italian words *a ventura*, meaning "by chance." Its name was actually stolen from a human-made mineral, now called Goldstone, that Aventurine naturally looks like. Goldstone was first called Aventurine because its creation happened by accident, when 17th-century glassmakers spilled copper flecks into a vat of glass. What we now call Aventurine has the same glassy quality and similar specks.

This reputation of being a stone of chance has given way to Aventurine's nickname, the Gambler's Stone. Aventurine is believed to be the luckiest stone in all games of chance. Thought to be 2.5 million years old, Aventurine has seen many uses. Ethiopian cultures used Aventurine to make different kinds of tools, including axes. Ancient Tibetans often adorned their statues' eyes with Aventurine because they believed it would increase its powers.

## WHAT CAN AVENTURINE DO FOR YOU?

Aventurine helps you create your own luck. Instead of believing that some people are luckier than others, take matters into your own hands. Use Aventurine as your lucky charm. Working with this crystal helps you become one of those "lucky people" by teaching you to find opportunity in every situation. Aventurine is your reminder that luck awaits you at every turn.

If you've ever gambled in Vegas and won, you know the feeling of invincibility that comes with an unexpected win. Aventurine helps you tap into that lucky feeling in any situation. Luck isn't something you have or don't have; it's a mind-set. Luck is a skill that you can practice and develop throughout your entire life. Part of being lucky is being in the right place at the right time, but it also requires seizing an opportunity when it's presented to you. Aventurine urges you to grab hold of sudden propositions or proposals. It helps to remove all doubts and negativity from your system so you are open to new possibilities and lucky breaks.

When you want to attract more luck in your life, the positive energy of Aventurine encourages you to say, "Yes!" to new prospects and follow up with "Where do I begin?" This stone reminds you to expect good things to come out of all your endeavors. In working with this crystal, you will find yourself being consistently in the right place at the right time—just like all the other lucky people you know. Aventurine helps you believe in your own luck, which, in turn, makes you luckier.

By staying receptive to positive change and open to new prospects, Aventurine increases your odds of success. Do you want to be lucky in love? In a job interview? Think of Aventurine as a luck amplifier in all your hopeful endeavors.

# I am lucky.

1   Hold your Aventurine and say out loud, "I am lucky," 3 times.

2   Carry it in your pocket or purse throughout the day and squeeze it, knowing that luck is on your side.

3   Whenever your Aventurine is with you, expect the best outcome in every situation.

# azurite

## improving mental focus

WHEN TO USE IT

When you feel distracted or unfocused

ORIGIN

Found in Australia, the Congo, Mexico, Morocco, Namibia,
the United States, and many other places

COLOR

Royal blue, often with green patches of Malachite within it

## HISTORY & LORE

Azurite's name is derived from the word *azure*, which means "sky blue." Azurite has long been used to give works of art their blue hue, especially during the Renaissance period. Even as far back as ancient Greece, Azurite was ground into a powder and used as pigment to dye clothes.

In ancient Egypt, Azurite was believed to raise the awareness of the high priests and priestesses to a godlike state. It was used as a pigment to paint the protective eye of Horus, the god of the sky, on their foreheads.

In ancient Chinese lore, Azurite was believed to open the door to spiritual heaven. Native Americans also believed Azurite to be a highly spiritual and sacred stone, used to connect to spirit guides.

## WHAT CAN AZURITE DO FOR YOU?

Azurite gets you focused. How many times have you tried to focus on a task only to find your mind wandering? Despite your best intentions, you just can't concentrate. Between your own mind chatter and the infinite distractions of social media, emails, and texts, staying focused can feel impossible. This is the time to use your Azurite.

Azurite helps you unclutter your mind and remove distraction. It is a stone of mental expansion, one that gives you the power to find ways to focus even when it doesn't seem possible. This crystal empowers you to find your focus by retraining your mind. It guides you to turn inward and stay on track instead of succumbing to diversions.

Azurite asks you to imagine what you would be capable of, if only you weren't distracted. Through working with Azurite, you can reconnect to what concentration feels like and be reminded of your ability to get focused whenever you choose. When you practice and train yourself to concentrate with the help of an Azurite crystal, it becomes second nature. Azurite enhances your ability to stay present with what you are doing. Once you get into the habit of consciously focusing, you can show up to anything and everything you do with an improved mental focus—from studying or working to having conversations with loved ones and much, much more.

Because focus comes from within, Azurite teaches you to rely only on your mind to get focused. It empowers you to not rely on the silence and stillness of your surroundings, but instead to create an environment within your own mind that supports your mental focus. When you learn to master your internal focus, the presence of external distractions will not throw you off. No matter where you are or when you need it, you have the power to get, and stay, focused.

# I am laser focused.

1   In a comfortable seated position, hold your Azurite in your hands and say out loud, "My mind is clear."

2   Set a timer for 1 minute. Hold your crystal up to your forehead, gently close your eyes, and begin to breathe deeply. Visualize the blue color of Azurite filling your mind and erasing any cluttered thoughts and mental fog.

3   Once the timer goes off, close your eyes again, hold your crystal to your forehead, and say out loud, "I am laser focused," 3 times.

4   Open your eyes to a more focused state of being.

# black kyanite

## cutting cords with toxic people

WHEN TO USE IT

When you feel drained by other people's energy

ORIGIN

Found in Brazil and India

COLOR

Black

## HISTORY & LORE

Legend says that Archangel Michael's "Sword of Truth" was made from a blade of Kyanite. As the protector and leader of all the angels, Michael and his sword were called upon to release fear, cut negative cords, and align with love.

Kyanite forms into unique bursts that appear as long streaks extending from a single point. It's Kyanite's broom-like shape that makes it an ideal tool for sweeping negative energetic debris from the aura and spirit.

Kyanite develops into a variety of different colors. Blue Kyanite is highly sought after by jewelers due to its gemlike, translucent quality when polished; Black Kyanite is most popular for metaphysical uses.

## WHAT CAN BLACK KYANITE DO FOR YOU?

Black Kyanite helps you cut cords with toxic people in your life. Though you might not be aware of it, you are constantly exposed to other people's energy—both positive and negative. When a person's energy is toxic, it negatively impacts you and your relationship with that person. Whether that person is a friend, a romantic partner, a co-worker, or even a stranger, Black Kyanite can help you identify their toxic energy.

Energetic cords are invisible attachments that bind you to another person's energy—often without either of you knowing it. This exchange of energy can happen after a random encounter with a stranger or a conversation with an acquaintance. If you notice that you can't shake someone's emotions off you or you suddenly feel a heaviness that you didn't have before, it's a clear sign that you need to cut the cords. Maybe it's a co-worker who has been making your work life miserable. Or it might be a frenemy who insults you in conversation and gossips behind your back. It could even be an ex-partner who still emotionally torments you. Black Kyanite will help you to assess where this dense energy is coming from and disconnect from that person's energy.

When you are ready to cut away the emotional bonds that no longer serve you, Black Kyanite is your crystal sword. It will slash off unwanted energy and cut away toxic ties. Rather than removing the person completely from your life, Black Kyanite allows you to break free from their negative energy so that your personal energy supply is not impacted. Its black color absorbs the negative vibrations once you cut them away from your energy field, leaving you to stand strong in your power.

# I cut the cords with all toxic relationships.

1   While holding your Black Kyanite in your dominant hand, visualize the toxic person you want to cut ties with standing in front of you, face-to-face.

2   Say out loud, "I cut the cords with _____."
    *(State the person's name.)*
    Repeat 2 more times.

3   Envision an energetic cord connecting you and that person. Move your Black Kyanite in a slicing motion, starting in front of your face and moving downward. Repeat this motion 3 times to cut the cord between you.

# black tourmaline

protecting yourself and your home

## HISTORY & LORE

Tourmaline has been valued since medieval times, but it wasn't until the late 1800s, when luxury jewelry retailer Tiffany & Co. propelled its demand, that it gained popularity.

Before it made a name for itself in popular culture, the power of Black Tourmaline was known only to those who worked with it. Many shamans of African, Aboriginal, and Native American tribes carried Tourmaline to protect themselves from danger.

In the 18th century, Dutch traders discovered another unique attribute of Black Tourmaline. Rubbing Black Tourmaline quickly causes the stone to become electrically charged—with a positive charge on one end of the stone and a negative charge on the other end. After making this discovery, the traders used the positively charged Black Tourmaline to collect the dust from their meerschaum pipes.

## WHAT CAN BLACK TOURMALINE DO FOR YOU?

Black Tourmaline protects you and your space from negative and unwanted energy. Have you ever felt like someone's bad mood was contagious? Or have you ever walked into a room and felt the lingering effects of a fight? What you've been feeling are left-over vibrations from negative energies. We are all susceptible to getting entangled in these lower frequencies, but Black Tourmaline helps you create an energetic force field around yourself to prevent "bad vibes" from leaving their impressions on you.

This powerful stone acts like a bodyguard against negative energy. Black Tourmaline takes the energetic hit so you don't have to. Whether you're at home or out in the world, this stone acts like a buffer to protect you from negative energy.

Protecting your space against darker energies is an essential component of energetic defense. Your home is your most sacred space, and while you can't control the energies outside of it, you can control what energy comes into it. You might not be aware of it, but you, your guests, and your family members are picking up energy from other people and places and bringing them back into your personal environment. Black Tourmaline will act as a protective shield when placed around your property or entryway, ensuring that negative energies get checked at the front door so that your home is protected, along with everyone in it.

In the same way that this crystal shields your home, it envelops you in a bubble of security against invasions of negative energy so you're protected against negativity wherever you go. For those stressful times when the car behind you won't stop honking, someone bumps into you on the street, or your co-worker takes their bad mood out on you, Black Tourmaline will supercharge your energetic personal protection. Keep it with you in your car, in your home, in your office, and on your person. With Black Tourmaline as your personal energetic bodyguard, you can move through your day feeling safe, secure, and protected from bad vibes and infectious bad moods.

# Protect me and my home.

1. Fill a small bowl with water and add a spoonful of sea salt. Salt adds another layer of protection as it absorbs negative energy.

2. Hold your Black Tourmaline in your hands and say out loud, "Protect me and my home," 3 times.

3. Place your crystal in the bowl and set it outside of your front door.

4. Once a month, take your Black Tourmaline out of the water and rinse it off. Flush the salt water down the toilet, and repeat steps 1–3.

# bloodstone

### get moving

**WHEN TO USE IT**

When you feel sluggish or lethargic

**ORIGIN**

Found in Australia, Brazil, China, India, and Russia

**COLOR**

Green and red

## HISTORY & LORE

Ancient civilizations long associated Bloodstone with blood. According to legend, a piece of Jasper was lying below Christ at his crucifixion. The blood that fell on the green Jasper was said to have forever stained it, creating Bloodstone. Mesopotamians believed that using Bloodstone could remedy problems with blood and the kidneys.

The Babylonians and ancient Egyptians both believed the stone increased personal strength and rendered one "invisible." Ancient warriors also believed that Bloodstone was intended to be carried into battle to stop bleeding when applied to a wound. The ancient Greeks and Romans carried Bloodstone during athletic competitions to bring endurance and assure victory.

## WHAT CAN BLOODSTONE DO FOR YOU?

Bloodstone gets your blood pumping and your body moving. When you're drained, depleted, and exhausted, even the smallest tasks can seem impossible. Working with Bloodstone is like a kick in the pants for those days when you feel extra tired and sluggish. This powerhouse stone encourages you to spring back into action rather than remain sedentary.

Bloodstone works to get the blood circulating within your body, helping to expel any stagnant energy that you may be holding on to. Working with this crystal creates a strong flow of energy in your body that contributes to a boost of physical power. By activating your physical state of being, Bloodstone helps you to feel more fully alive. Let this stone reinvigorate you on a cellular level so that you can move through your day with more vitality.

Not only does your body respond to this crystal's energy frequency, but it also reacts to Bloodstone's energizing colors. The way its bright green and red colors fuse together turns your life force back on. While the green coloring connects with the energy of physical growth, the red droplets bring in vitality and strength. By infusing your body with these energies, Bloodstone gets you on your feet and ready to go.

Making movement a priority is a daily choice, and Bloodstone inspires you to more consciously incorporate it into your life. Maybe you've been working yourself to the bone and are having trouble simply getting through the day. Maybe you are so busy with family that you've forgotten to make time to move your body. Or maybe you've been behind your computer for the entire day and your body feels stiff and sore. Whatever the reason you've disconnected from movement, Bloodstone prompts you to stop making excuses and start taking the time you need to get the energy flowing in your body. Let Bloodstone act as your trainer, cheering you on to get up and get moving.

# I get up and move.

1   Hold your Bloodstone in your hands and say out loud, "I get up and move," 3 times.

2   Find a way to get moving! Take the stairs instead of the elevator. Go for a quick walk outside. Dance to your favorite song. Or head to your favorite workout class—whatever gets your blood pumping.

3   Carry your Bloodstone with you in your bra or pocket as you move.

# blue lace agate

## releasing stress

WHEN TO USE IT

When you feel stressed out or overwhelmed

ORIGIN

Found only in southern Africa

COLOR

Bands of pale blue and white

## HISTORY & LORE

The name *Blue Lace Agate* comes from the beautiful white lines that cut across the sky-blue stone and create a lace-like pattern. Blue Lace Agate is one of the rarest crystals on the planet because it is only found in one mine in Namibia. It was discovered in 1962 by prospector George Swanson and was mined by hand until 1977. Subsequently, the mine closed in 2016. The blue hue of Blue Lace Agate depends on the depth from which the stone was mined. In general, the deeper the mine, the bluer the stone. Only about 30 percent of mined pieces of Blue Lace Agate weigh more than one kilogram, so large pieces of this crystal are very rare.

## WHAT CAN BLUE LACE AGATE DO FOR YOU?

Blue Lace Agate helps you relieve stress. Although stress is inevitable, being able to self-soothe and reduce your stress levels can improve your mood, boost your physical health, and allow you to be more productive. In the midst of a stressful situation, reach for Blue Lace Agate to help you return to a state of calm.

At first glance, Blue Lace Agate might remind you of the ocean or the sky. This stone encourages you to sit back, relax, and breathe a little deeper. Working with Blue Lace Agate brings you to ask yourself, *What exactly is creating my stress?* Instead of allowing yourself to worry about all that can go wrong, Blue Lace Agate supports calm and rational thought. When you connect with this crystal, you can almost see your stress floating away, drifting off into the distance. The sense of relief that results from connecting with Blue Lace Agate will help to bring about a sense of tranquility so you can move through the stress and come out healthier and happier on the other side.

Whatever the source, Blue Lace Agate can help you pinpoint your triggers so you can better manage them before stress paralyzes you. Some stressors can be alleviated quickly, while others take time and discipline to reduce. In either situation, Blue Lace Agate is a tool to help you learn to manage and reduce your stress levels.

Blue Lace Agate helps you release stress so you can stop a situation from getting out of control. It emits calming and soothing vibrations that can ease your stressed-out spirit. This tranquil blue crystal can shift your state of mind from chaos to calm. From this place, you can calmly approach the situation at hand and find a stress-free way to get through it.

# I am calm.

1   Press a piece of Blue Lace Agate into the underside of one of your wrlsts with your opposite thumb.

2   As you apply light pressure, say out loud, "I am calm," 9 times.

3   Carry your Blue Lace Agate in your pocket or purse throughout the day.

4   Repeat steps 1 and 2 whenever your stress arises.

# carnelian

## unlocking your creative potential

WHEN TO USE IT

When you want to tap into your creative nature

ORIGIN

Found in Brazil, India, Scotland, the United States, and many other places

COLOR

Reddish orange

## HISTORY & LORE

Ancient Byzantine and Assyrian cultures used Carnelian to foster courage, both in battle as well as during performances. Carnelian was believed to help timid speakers become eloquent and bold. The ancient Egyptians believed that wearing Carnelian added a sense of vitality to the spirit and body. They referred to Carnelian as the "setting sun." For these reasons, Carnelian was included in King Tut's pectoral and death mask. Because of its orange hues, they also likened Carnelian to the fertile menstrual blood of the mother goddess, Isis.

Carnelian has been identified as one of the first of 12 stones in the breastplate of Aaron, the elder brother of Moses. It is also one of the 12 gemstones that lined the walls of heaven in Revelation.

## WHAT CAN CARNELIAN DO FOR YOU?

Carnelian unlocks your creative potential. Whether you realize it or not, everyone is born with the ability to be creative—including you! Carnelian helps to unleash an infinite number of ways to tap into your creative side.

This crystal's orangey-red color ignites a fire within you that brings out your passion and imagination. It draws out the bold, adventure-seeking, risk-taking part of you. Working with Carnelian helps you think outside of the box, push your personal boundaries, and tap into your true creative potential. To get your creative juices flowing, Carnelian helps spark the joy and excitement that a creative endeavor can bring about.

Tapping into your creative nature is less about the outcome and more about the process. It's less about what you create, and more about how you feel when you're brainstorming, imagining, and creating. Carnelian helps ignite your creative process, not only in that one specific instance but in all areas of your life. The feelings that you experience while working with Carnelian carry over into your professional life, your personal life, your relationships, and more.

If you find yourself creatively blocked, take a deeper look at what's stopping you. Overthinking and overanalyzing can prevent you from creating freely. When you are caught up in your thoughts, Carnelian takes you out of your head and connects you with your creative impulses. Stop waiting for your creative muse to come along! Instead, embrace the passionate energy of Carnelian. Is fear of failure a debilitating block to your creativity? Before you've even started on your creative endeavor, do you find yourself wanting to quit because it's not going to be good enough? Or maybe you hold yourself back because you're afraid of putting yourself out there. Regardless of what is preventing you from empowering your creative nature, Carnelian will give you the confidence to pursue your creative journey.

# I unlock my creative potential.

1   When you need to tap into your creativity, hold your Carnelian in your hands and say out loud, "I unlock my creative potential," 3 times.

2   Close your eyes and visualize the fiery energy of Carnelian igniting your creativity and acting as the key to unlock the creative potential that lives within you.

3   Take the first step and start your creative act.

4   Every time you want to infuse more creativity into what you're doing, repeat steps 1-3.

# celestite

sleeping well

WHEN TO USE IT

When you're having trouble sleeping

ORIGIN

Found in Egypt, Madagascar, Mexico, Poland, and the United Kingdom

COLOR

Blue

## HISTORY & LORE

The subtle, baby-blue hue of this stone is where Celestite got its name. Celestite comes from the Latin word meaning "heavenly." When it was originally discovered in 1791, it was named Fasriger Schwerspath. And that mouthful didn't get much better in 1797, when it was renamed Schwefelsaurer Strontianite Aus Pennsylvania. The next year, thankfully, it was named Zoelestine, which is the German spelling that's based off the Latin word for "of the sky." And that's how it finally came to be Celestine, which later became the now popularized Celestite. Some have reverted back to using the name *Celestine*, but most still call it Celestite—because we have to stick with one name at some point!

## WHAT CAN CELESTITE DO FOR YOU?

Celestite helps you sleep well. If you were to imagine what sleep looks like, it would be very similar to the cloudlike blue-and-white appearance of a Celestite crystal. This crystal's energy is as soothing and serene as its appearance. The soft blue color brings gentle, calming energy into your bedroom to usher you into a deep sleep. At the same time, its jagged edges and ice-like quality pierce through heavy, dense, or dark energy that can prevent peaceful sleep. This combination of soft, effective energy is exactly what you need to help eliminate restlessness.

When stress, worry, fear, or any other negative state of mind prevents you from falling asleep, think of Celestite as your comfort crystal. Just like the security blanket or stuffed animal that you might have held as a child, this crystal emits a reassuring energy that helps you feel safe and secure by canceling out stress and tension. Once your mind, body, and spirit are comforted, you can drift off to dreamland. Celestite is also a powerful tool for combatting disturbing dreams or panic-filled nightmares that can disrupt your rest. Its calming energy will clear your mind, dispelling negative thoughts that might haunt you throughout the night. Free of that mental chatter, you can sleep soundly until morning.

In the same way that Celestite works to bring comfort and calm to your mind, body, and spirit, it also infuses your bedroom with sleep-enhancing vibes. Your bedroom should be your sanctuary, but when leftover energy or frustration from your day finds its way in, it can disrupt your rest. Bring Celestite into your bedroom to emit a calm, soothing frequency and infuse the space with tranquility and peace. This will simultaneously transform dark energy leftover from the day into lighter vibrations. It clears away any remaining negative energy so that you are enveloped by calming, sleep-inducing energy. With Celestite infusing positive frequencies into the air, you can lay your head on your pillow and rest easy through the night.

# I sleep soundly.

1  Start by decluttering your nightstand. The clearer your nightstand, the clearer your mind.

2  Hold your Celestite in your hands and say out loud, "I sleep soundly," 7 times.

3  Place your Celestite on your nightstand. Gaze at its soothing color and breathe deeply as you drift off to sleep.

4  Once a month, place your crystal outside in the Sun for 4 hours to cleanse.

# chrysocolla

## starting fresh

WHEN TO USE IT

When you're ready to start over

ORIGIN

Found in Australia, England, Israel, Mexico,
the United States, and many other places

COLOR

A mixture of blue and green

## HISTORY & LORE

Chrysocolla was named by the Greek philosopher Theophrastus after the Greek words meaning "gold" and "glue." This stone, full of copper ore, was often used to solder gold. It was also used during the Renaissance to create a pigment for paint. To do this, they had to grind up the Chrysocolla crystal into a fine powder. The green powder created by ground-up Chrysocolla stone was also used by Roman Emperor Nero. Because Nero belonged to the elite green faction of Rome, he would dust the arenas of his chariot races with green Chrysocolla powder.

Legend says that those who carried Chrysocolla with them would experience more creativity and femininity. It is believed that Cleopatra carried this stone with her at all times. It is also believed to have made those with volatile tempers become more tolerant. Native Americans believe Chrysocolla can bring calm to tense situations.

## WHAT CAN CHRYSOCOLLA DO FOR YOU?

Chrysocolla gives you a fresh start. This crystal carries with it the energy of New Year's Day—the excitement of a new beginning. But you don't have to wait until January 1 to make a fresh start. Every day can be the first day of the life you want to live. Chrysocolla will motivate you by stimulating new ideas and fresh perspectives. It is a crystal of self-reflection and self-awareness. It beckons you to consider what needs changing and empowers you to go after it. Instead of settling for the way things are, let Chrysocolla give you a fresh new outlook for how things can be.

Chrysocolla emits a soft, yet constant, energy that nurtures your development. This crystal will not let you settle for "good enough." It carries within it a confident and affirming energy, reminding you that you are capable of whatever you put your mind to. In tandem with positive affirmations, Chrysocolla draws out negativity from the mind, body, and spirit to make more room for an "out with the old, in with the new" perspective in every aspect of your life.

Have you been going through life on autopilot? Have you been wanting to start fresh, but you just cannot seem to make it happen? Have you been avoiding change at all costs? The gentle guidance of Chrysocolla will get you excited about the possibilities ahead, allowing you to move past fear, doubt, or lack of motivation. It will support you on your path to creating the life you love.

It takes courage and bravery to start fresh. Chrysocolla reminds you not to fear the unknown, but to embrace it. Are you looking for a new relationship? A career change? Is a move on the horizon? This crystal helps you identify the areas of your life that are ready for change and supports your journey toward a new beginning. Stop waiting for tomorrow, or next month, or next year—start today with the help of Chrysocolla.

# I start fresh today.

1   Give your closet a deep clean. Organize and throw away old clothes. This is symbolic of letting go of the past.

2   Create empty space in your closet. This makes room for a fresh start.

3   Hold your Chrysocolla in your hands and say out loud, "I start fresh today," 3 times.

4   Place your Chrysocolla in your closet. Whenever you see it, be reminded that today is a new day.

# chrysoprase

connecting with those around you

WHEN TO USE IT

When you feel disconnected from the people around you

ORIGIN

Found in Australia, Brazil, Russia, and the United States

COLOR

Light to deep green

## HISTORY & LORE

Chrysoprase was said to be worn by Alexander the Great in his armor when he led his men into battle. Legend says that while he was bathing in the Euphrates, a serpent came along, bit the stone off him, and tossed it in the water. After that, he never won a battle.

Frederick the Great of Prussia had snuff boxes carved out of Chrysoprase and gave them as gifts to his family. In fact, it is said that one of these boxes actually saved his life when it deflected a bullet during a battle in the Seven Years' War.

Many churches and cathedrals around Europe have cups made of Chrysoprase, professing them to be the Holy Grail.

## WHAT CAN CHRYSOPRASE DO FOR YOU?

Chrysoprase brings you back to real connection. If you've lost touch with the people around you, either because your relationships have been maintained only online or because you're too busy to acknowledge the people around you throughout your day, then Chrysoprase is your crystal. It encourages you to make meaningful, real-life, in-person connections with others every single day.

Chrysoprase reminds you that connection is a two-way street. You have to open yourself up and put yourself out there if you want that energy in return. Chrysoprase opens your heart to new relationships and empowers you to reach out to others to get the heartfelt connection you need. Instead of feeling isolated or lonely, this crystal urges you to find ways to connect with the people in your life—from your friends and family to co-workers and even strangers.

This crystal gives you the push you need to ask an old friend out to lunch or invite a new acquaintance to take a walk. It urges you to call your loved ones and to introduce yourself to the people you meet throughout the day. Chrysoprase pushes you to make an effort to connect with others in small or big ways every day. Once you've started making yourself available to others, Chrysoprase takes it one step further by empowering you to create new habits in order to receive more love and support in your life. What can you do every day to strengthen your sense of human connection? With your heart wide open, Chrysoprase teaches you to welcome and receive the different ways that connection shows up.

Working with Chrysoprase also encourages you to reconnect with the people and things you have detached yourself from. Are you wishing for a romantic connection? Are you missing your family? Has it been too long since your last girls' night? Use Chrysoprase to reignite your desire to connect with others and prioritize those forms of connection that have been pushed aside.

# I connect with those around me.

1   Once a month, plan an outing to be more present and connected. Turn your phone off or put it in airplane mode. Bring your Chrysoprase with you.

2   Hold your Chrysoprase in your hand and say out loud, "I connect with those around me."

3   Every time you feel the urge to check your phone, connect with your Chrysoprase instead. Use this time to focus your energy on face-to-face conversations with friends, family, and co-workers.

# citrine

choosing happiness

**WHEN TO USE IT**

When you're feeling down

**ORIGIN**

Found in Brazil, Madagascar, Russia, and the United States

**COLOR**

Yellow to orange and light brown

## HISTORY & LORE

Citrine's name is derived from the French word *citron*, meaning "lemon," due to its color. Citrine has long been remarked upon for its subtle, honeyed beauty. Though the stone has an abundant history of being used in jewelry by ancient civilizations, Citrine is actually very rare today. Most Citrine seen on the market is actually Amethyst that has been heat treated to achieve a yellow hue.

Real Citrine was used in the jewelry of Greek and Roman civilizations dating back to the 1st century A.D. Citrine was also featured in the flamingo brooch of the Duchess of Windsor and in Bulgari's Cerchi earrings.

Known as "the merchant's stone," Citrine is said to bring prosperity when placed in a cash register.

## WHAT CAN CITRINE DO FOR YOU?

Citrine helps you choose to be happy. If you live by the saying "I'll be happy when . . . ," then you have fallen into the happiness trap. The truth is that happiness comes from within. It isn't contingent upon external circumstances, but rather how you decide to see these circumstances. You have the power to choose whether or not to be happy every day! Working with Citrine makes that choice a little easier. Tuning in to your happiness is like standing in the Sun, and the sunny energy of Citrine emits a frequency that connects you with that light, happy feeling. Even just by looking at this crystal, you will feel its sunshine energy. Citrine's bright energy stimulates higher vibrational frequencies within you. Working with Citrine offers a contagious exchange of uplifting vibrations, infusing you with higher levels of happiness and joy.

When you feel stuck in lower vibrational frequencies, and happiness seems like an impossible choice to make, Citrine can shine a light and help burn away any darkness in your life. By working with Citrine, you can adopt its sunny energy. Citrine does not hold any darkness and is incapable of emitting negative frequencies. By carrying only high vibrations, Citrine inspires you to do the same. It guides you away from the darkness of your mind and reminds you that you have the ability to tap into your happiness—anytime, anywhere.

Citrine reminds you that not all days will be the brightest and happiest, just like not all Citrine crystals are as bright and sunny as others. Whether it's dim or bright, each day is an opportunity to find your sunny disposition within. Instead of relying on other people or external circumstances to make you happy, let the energy of a Citrine crystal remind you to choose to be happy every single day.

# I choose to be happy.

1  When you wake up, open the shades, crack the window, and let in the sunlight.

2  Hold your Citrine in your hand and say out loud, "I choose to be happy," 3 times.

3  Place your Citrine in your pocket or purse, and carry it with you throughout the day. Every time you see it, remind yourself to choose happiness.

# clear quartz

## gaining clarity

**WHEN TO USE IT**

When you are unclear on what you want

**ORIGIN**

Found all over the world

**COLOR**

Clear

92

## HISTORY & LORE

Many ancient cultures around the world have their own Clear Quartz myths. In Europe during the Middle Ages, Clear Quartz crystal balls were said to give clairvoyants the ability to predict the future. Native South American cultures believed that Clear Quartz crystals carved into skulls held the spirits of their ancestors.

Ancient Egyptians used Clear Quartz crystal in monuments, as they believed it would channel the energy from the sky, Sun, and stars. According to ancient Japanese mythology, Clear Quartz was the physical form of white dragon's breath. Dragons were symbols of generosity and benevolence in ancient Japan, so these myths regarded Clear Quartz as a symbol of perfection.

## WHAT CAN CLEAR QUARTZ DO FOR YOU?

Clear Quartz gives you clarity. When someone asks you what you want in life, do you have trouble answering? If so, there may be a few factors involved. When you don't truly know yourself, it is difficult to know what you want. Your goals and ambitions can also be overshadowed by expectations or dreams projected onto you by others— family, friends, co-workers, and society at large. Your desires may have been either pushed aside or crushed under the weight of the world. Working with Clear Quartz will help to drown out the noise so you can get crystal clear on what you really, truly want.

This crystal illuminates the path to soul-level clarity. First, you must get clear on the path you want to take. Clear Quartz helps by clearing your mind to bring to light your authentic desires. A spam filter for your mind, Clear Quartz will help you scan for mental "garbage" and delete it. It allows you to rise above your erratic thoughts, insecurity, or confusion to an elevated state. With a clear state of mind, Clear Quartz helps you strengthen your connection to your truest, highest self and zero in on what you truly want. From this aligned state of being, you can work with Clear Quartz to program your mind to bring what you want to life.

Use Clear Quartz as a visual for the kind of clarity you are capable of achieving. As an energetic prescription for 20/20 vision, Clear Quartz helps you see yourself and your path more clearly when you are foggy and don't know which direction to turn. For all those times when you feel lost, unsure, and misguided, reach for your Clear Quartz to get the clarity you need.

# I am crystal clear.

1   In a comfortable seated position, hold your Clear Quartz in your hand and say out loud, "I am crystal clear," 3 times.

2   Still holding your crystal, gently close your eyes, and ask yourself, *What is one thing I need clarity on today?*

3   Meditate on that thought for 3 minutes.

4   Say out loud, "I am crystal clear," 3 more times.

5   Carry your Clear Quartz in your pocket or purse throughout the day. Take it out and hold it in your hands during moments when you need more clarity.

# epidote

## healing from betrayal

WHEN TO USE IT

When you feel betrayed

ORIGIN

Found in Brazil, Bulgaria, France, Myanmar, Norway,
Pakistan, and the United States

COLOR

Ranges from yellow green to pistachio green

96

## HISTORY & LORE

Epidote forms into a variety of distinctly unique shapes. When Epidote develops into complex, interconnected prisms, it becomes highly prized by gem and rock collectors. The most sought after variety of Epidote has a translucent pistachio-green luster.

Its name comes from the Greek word for "increase," due to the way the stone seems to build out in one direction as it develops. This may explain why in medieval times, physicians prescribed crushed Epidote powder as a tonic to help "increase" overall physical well-being. It is still believed in metaphysical circles to be a stone for increasing the attraction of whatever energy you put out. For this reason, Epidote is also referred to as a karmic stone.

## WHAT CAN EPIDOTE DO FOR YOU?

Epidote helps you heal from betrayal. Whatever type of betrayal you have experienced, the first step to healing is to process your feelings. Epidote nudges you to release the toxic emotions associated with the painful memories of disloyalty.

When you have been betrayed, it can be difficult to discuss your feelings, even with your family and your closest friends. You might feel embarrassed or ashamed for having allowed yourself to be misled. This is the time to use Epidote. Speak to it. Talking about your hurt with your crystal will help to diffuse toxic emotions. Epidote can help you to move past the painful experience by acknowledging the pain. It acts like a sponge, absorbing anger, resentment, hurt, confusion, frustration, and disappointment. Epidote reminds you to stop giving the old betrayal any more attention. It's time to move forward.

Rather than keeping protective barriers around your heart, Epidote encourages you to start to break them down so you can open yourself up to love and connection with others. Working with Epidote gives you the strength to face the betrayal head on so that it no longer holds power over you. It will help you get to a place where you are ready to tear down the walls around your heart and start to rebuild your ability to trust.

Epidote encourages you to stop thinking about how someone betrayed you and instead concentrate on how you are treating yourself. Are you blaming yourself for being betrayed? Is your anger preventing you from enjoying your life? Are you consumed with plotting revenge? All these emotions are preventing you from healing and moving forward. Epidote absorbs these negative feelings so you can begin the healing process. It's time to shift your thoughts away from the betrayal and focus on the present, where you are ready to trust again.

# I am healing from betrayal.

1  Hold your Epidote in your hands and say out loud, "I am healing from betrayal," 9 times.

2  Still holding your crystal in your hands, think about the person who betrayed you. Say out loud all the raw emotions that come to your mind. Express your anger. Scream. Cry. Let your Epidote absorb and remove your hurt emotions.

3  Put your Epidote out in the Sun for 4 hours to cleanse.

4  Repeat steps 1–3 as often as needed.

# fluorite

## making wishes

On your birthday and anytime you want to make a wish!

**ORIGIN**

Found in Brazil, China, Europe, Mexico, and many other places

**COLOR**

Ranges from colorless to purple, green, and yellow

## HISTORY & LORE

Fluorite was named from the Latin word *fluere*, meaning "to flow," stemming from Fluorite's ability to act as a flux between metals. Because of its rainbow coloring, Fluorite was thought to house rainbows.

In China, Fluorite has been sculpted into ornate vessels for over three centuries. Ancient Egyptians carved Fluorite to resemble scarabs and used it for statues of deities. Ancient Romans used Fluorite for decoration. In fact, Pliny the Elder, an ancient Roman scholar and historian, loved Fluorite so much that he named it one of his favorite minerals.

One of the more spectacular attributes of this stone is called *fluorescence*, and refers to Fluorite's ability to glow in the dark after having been exposed to UV light.

## WHAT CAN FLUORITE DO FOR YOU?

Fluorite encourages you to make wishes. As a child, you were encouraged to make wishes on birthdays, on stars, on pennies thrown into fountains. You were excited to share your dreams with anyone who was willing to listen, even your biggest and most extravagant ones! But when was the last time you made a wish as an adult? When was the last time you felt confident enough to share your wishes with someone? If the process of making a wish or talking about it out loud makes you feel silly, Fluorite can help you get back in touch with your sense of hopefulness. Fluorite's energy is a shooting star or cluster of burning birthday candles beckoning you to make that wish!

This crystal's rainbow energy wants you to dream big and believe in the magic of the universe. It motivates you to get in touch with your imagination. Fluorite can help you connect to your highest potential and wish for all you want in life. Think of holding on to Fluorite as holding on to your dreams. This crystal begs you to ask yourself, *If my imagination had no boundaries, what would I wish for?*

Fluorite's colorful and dreamy appearance fills your spirit with peace, stability, and positivity so that you are comfortable with your bold aspirations. It gives even the most practical version of yourself permission to believe that anything is possible, and invites you to indulge in your fantasies. Use Fluorite when you need to connect with the wonder and awe of the impossible so you can embrace even the most extraordinary possibilities. No dream is too big, so let your imagination run free and discover what you truly wish for. Once you're clear on what you want, this crystal expands your mind to believe that your wishes can come true. Sending your wish out into the world is the first step to making it a reality, and Fluorite will help you do just that.

CRYSTAL INTENTION

# My wish comes true.

CRYSTAL PRACTICE

1 Hold your Fluorite in your dominant hand and say your wish out loud 3 times.

2 Say out loud, "My wish comes true," 9 times.

3 Place your crystal on your windowsill where the sunlight will hit it every day. Every time you see your crystal, think of your wish and know it will come true.

# garnet

igniting passion

## HISTORY & LORE

According to some interpretations of the Old Testament, the light beaming from Garnet was used to steer Noah's ark out of the darkness. Many ancient civilizations valued Garnet as a symbol of protection. The ancient Romans used Garnets to adorn their armor because they were thought to represent Mars, the god of war. During the Middle Ages, it was said that wearing Garnet would keep the wearer from being poisoned. Medieval soldiers wore Garnets for luck when going into battle, and King Solomon was believed to wear Garnet to ensure victory.

Garnet was also used in ancient times for romantic purposes. It was known as "the Conqueror's stone," for its ability to aid in romantic conquests. King Louis XIV is reported to have placed Garnets directly on top of his genitals to remedy a lack of sex drive and impotence.

## WHAT CAN GARNET DO FOR YOU?

Garnet ignites your passion. Passion is like a muscle: you need to use it to keep it strong. Working with Garnet will help you strengthen your sense of passion in every situation so you can live a full and vibrant life.

The crystal recipe for passion is to be present and enthusiastic. Passion lives in your heart. When you are present and bring a heartfelt enthusiasm and joy to everything you do, you start to experience passion. Garnet's deep-red coloring gets you jazzed up about what you're doing and gets your heart involved.

Garnet reminds you that passion is not external; it comes from within. Passion exists *wherever* you decide to create it. Garnet helps you get to the bottom of what is keeping you from feeling passionate. If you don't feel passionate about your career, Garnet empowers you to ask, *Why?* Perhaps it's because you don't feel stimulated by your work or you don't feel that what you are doing is important. Either way, Garnet will inspire you to change your attitude. It infuses your spirit with enthusiasm and eagerness.

If you've lost the passion in your relationship, ask yourself, *How can I show up differently?* Work with Garnet to reinvigorate your relationship with love and lust, instead of exhaustion and separation. Garnet helps to spice things up in the bedroom. Maybe you've settled into a routine and the sex has gone stale. It's time to bring back a sense of fervor. Let the rich, passionate red of Garnet help to spark the flames of desire.

If personal passion is what you are missing, work with Garnet to rekindle a sense of excitement for yourself. Think about the books you buy, the music you listen to, how and with whom you spend your free time. Maybe you are passionate about your health or travel or your favorite sports team. Use Garnet to identify all the parts of your life that you are already passionate about and to ignite passion in other parts of your life, as well.

# I am passionate.

1. Hold your Garnet in your non-writing hand and write down 10 things that you are passionate about. These can be things that you love, like, or enjoy doing.

2. Still holding your Garnet, now ask yourself, *Which one of these things brings me the most passion? Which one of them reignites my excitement for life?* Circle that one thing.

3. With that one thing in mind, say out loud, "I am passionate," 3 times.

4. Place your list in your bedroom with your Garnet atop as a reminder to incorporate more of that one thing into your life.

# golden healer quartz

dealing with family conflict

WHEN TO USE IT

When you're navigating challenging family dynamics

ORIGIN

Found all over the world

COLOR

Yellow to golden and translucent

## HISTORY & LORE

This variety of Quartz takes on its sunny hues from inclusions of iron oxide. It is also sometimes called Yellow Hematoid Quartz. The word *Hematoid* is a reference to the iron inclusions within the stone. In Latin, *hema* means "blood," and *toid* means "to resemble," so Hematoid translates to "resembling blood." However, Yellow Hematoid Quartz has other mineral inclusions that cause it to appear more yellow or orange than blood red.

## WHAT CAN GOLDEN HEALER QUARTZ DO FOR YOU?

Golden Healer Quartz helps you stay in control when dealing with challenging family dynamics. The energy of Golden Healer Quartz is not intended to heal your relationship with your family, but rather to help you cope with it. It offers you the emotional distance and perspective you need to stop yourself from falling into the old traps of the family drama paradigm. This crystal reminds you to be the one who shows up in a calmer and more open state of mind, and it calls on you to be the healer. With the clear mental state that this crystal provides, you will be able to partake in open communication and make rational decisions.

Golden Healer Quartz reminds you not to take things so personally. Whenever something is said or done that triggers an argument or negative reaction, take a moment to step away and reconnect with the energy of Golden Healer Quartz. Rather than saying something you'll only wind up regretting, it's better to remove yourself from the situation and use your crystal to calm yourself down and prevent tensions from escalating. Golden Healer Quartz will help to raise your vibration to a higher state so that you can have better control of your own actions.

When you need to shift toxic behaviors and responses to interactions with family members, Golden Healer Quartz is here to help. This crystal encourages you to find a healthier reaction to conflict or tension. If you're feeling anxious about a family gathering, the soothing energy of Golden Healer Quartz can help you to regain control of your emotions and get centered. It calms the deep layers of your spirit so you can address frustration or resentment in a more mindful way. It is especially beneficial to work with when you're going through a separation or divorce. It brings stability to chaos and allows you to move through difficult transitions with a higher perspective.

This crystal teaches you to shift the negative patterns of your family dynamics by changing the way you show up to gatherings. Your family members won't change because of this crystal, but you can change the way you interact with them.

# I am nonreactive to family conflict.

1   Before you head to a family gathering, hold your Golden Healer Quartz and say out loud, "I am nonreactive to family conflict," 3 times.

2   Bring your Golden Healer Quartz with you as a touchstone to help you remain calm.

3   Every time you feel your emotions getting out of control, squeeze your crystal. Let it be a reminder to not react to family triggers.

# hematite

### getting grounded

**WHEN TO USE IT**

When you're feeling scattered or unsettled

**ORIGIN**

Found in Brazil, Canada, England, the United States,
Venezuela, and many other places

**COLOR**

Steel gray, sometimes with red streaks running through it

---
112

## HISTORY & LORE

Hematite's name is derived from the Greek word *haima*, meaning "blood." This stone is known for connecting the body to the Earth. Ancient Romans associated Hematite with Mars, the god of war. Many warriors, including ancient Greeks, Romans, and Native Americans, used crushed Hematite on their bodies to create a red-paint-like appearance thought to keep them safe in battle. Hematite was believed to make warriors invulnerable and give them courage and strength. During the Paleolithic era, early humans created cave paintings using the red pigment from ground-up Hematite.

Hematite was also used for medicinal purposes in ancient times. In Mesopotamia, Hematite was used to cool the blood. Similarly, in ancient Egypt, Hematite was recommended for treating inflammation because of its iron oxide properties.

## WHAT CAN HEMATITE DO FOR YOU?

Hematite grounds the mind, body, and spirit. Nature is one of the most powerful grounding forces there is, and because of the energy of the Earth contained within crystals, holding Hematite can support you in getting grounded. When you feel like the rug has been pulled out from under you, Hematite can help you get back on your feet again.

Hematite has a metallic silver sheen to it as a result of its high iron content. Holding this dense stone offers stability, anchoring you to the Earth. Hematite's magnetic pull to the Earth roots you into the stillness of the present moment. It helps you get connected to the ground beneath you so you can feel centered, supported, and secure.

Working with Hematite teaches you to be in control of your mental and emotional states, even in unsettling situations. This stone helps you build a strong foundation so you can move through turbulent times with more grace and ease. With the grounding energy that Hematite provides, you will be less likely to react to stressful circumstances or feel diminished by overpowering people. Just as it helps you stand your ground in the face of oncoming stress, Hematite also encourages you to approach everything in life from a grounded place. This crystal reminds you to be slow and steady in all your endeavors. It teaches you to take it one step at a time so you get to where you want to go without losing your footing.

Have you recently moved? Did you just lose a job or start a new one? Do you feel as though you are running around all day without a minute to regroup? For those times when you feel like you just can't find your foundation, Hematite will be there to support you. Its grounding energy is there to help you feel safe, centered, and secure no matter where you are or what you are confronting.

# I am grounded.

1  Stand with your feet slightly apart and firmly planted on the ground.

2  Hold a piece of Hematite in each hand, close your eyes, and take 3 deep breaths.

3  As you breathe, visualize yourself as a tall, strong tree. See the roots of the tree—a few inches in diameter—growing from the sole of each foot and spiraling down into the core of the Earth to create a solid foundation.

4  Say out loud, "I am grounded," 3 times.

5  Open your eyes. You are now grounded.

# iolite

eliminating debt

WHEN TO USE IT

When you want to get out of debt

ORIGIN

Found in India, Madagascar, Myanmar, South Africa,
Sri Lanka, and Tanzania

COLOR

Dark blue to indigo

## HISTORY & LORE

Iolite is named from the Greek word *ios*, meaning "violet." Also known as Water Sapphire, Iolite is the blue, gem-quality variety of the stone Cordierite. While Cordierite develops into many shades, from bluish green to gray violet, Iolite comes exclusively in a deep shade of blue. Because it can be formed into many shapes, it is often used in jewelry.

Iolite is also known as the Viking Compass Stone. Ancient Viking navigators were said to have used pieces of Iolite to locate the Sun by reducing glare and creating polarizing filters. Iolite was also used by Nordic mariners to pinpoint the Sun and guide them at sea, which allowed them to travel to the new world and back without GPS technology.

## WHAT CAN IOLITE DO FOR YOU?

Iolite helps to eliminate debt. Instead of living in shame or regret, work with Iolite to climb your way out. This stone unites the mind, body, and spirit, emboldening you to reevaluate your financial life and become more financially responsible. Iolite pushes you to explore your behaviors surrounding money so you can eliminate debt once and for all.

Iolite assists in breaking the cycle of debt by getting to the heart of the matter. It encourages you to address the issues that got you into financial trouble in the first place. How did you get here? Maybe it was an accumulation of honest mistakes. Maybe it was because you never felt worthy enough and overcompensated by buying things. Whatever the reason, the uplifting vibrations of Iolite can help you transform your relationship with money and rebalance your budget.

Connecting with the raw honesty of Iolite helps you to prioritize your spending. When making a purchase, ask yourself, *Do I really need to spend this amount?* Iolite helps you to rethink your purchases before you go through with them. Are you eating out when you could be saving money by buying food to cook at home? Do you have to buy a new dress for that wedding, or could you wear one that you that already own? Iolite lends you the courage to say "no" to impulsive and unnecessary purchases so you can stop debt from piling up.

Not only does Iolite help you make better financial decisions, it also reinforces a stronger sense of self-worth. A confident you can begin to develop a healthier relationship with money. Iolite helps you to love and value yourself unconditionally, so you don't overcompensate by buying unnecessary items. It shifts your mentality away from constantly needing more to being content. Learning to be satisfied with what you have instead of always being worried about what you don't can dramatically shift your money mind-set.

Connect with your crystal financial advisor, Iolite, to take a more mindful approach to your finances on your journey to eliminate debt.

# I will be debt-free.

1  Hold your Iolite in your hand and say out loud, "I will be debt-free," 3 times.

2  Place your Iolite on top of your credit cards.

3  For three months, pay non-necessity expenses in cash. It is said that paying with cash makes you more present and connected to the purchase.

4  With every purchase, ask yourself, *Do I need to spend this money?*

# jade

living a prosperous life

WHEN TO USE IT

When you want to enhance your success in all areas of your life

ORIGIN

Found in Canada, China, Mexico, New Zealand,
the United States, and many other places

COLOR

Ranges from light to dark green

## HISTORY & LORE

For centuries, Jade has been thought to bring good fortune. Cultures all over the world believe that Jade represents a wealth of virtues, including happiness, courage, purity, longevity, and wisdom. The ancient Chinese belief that Jade protected against death and decay led to the creation of Jade burial suits. These suits were composed of thousands of Jade tiles connected by wire to encase the bodies of royal members of a dynasty before being placed in their tombs.

In China, it is also believed that wearing Jade acts as a protective shield against many kinds of misfortune. Jade, the Chinese advise, should be worn and never tucked away in a box, lest it turn white and die. If your Jade becomes chipped, it is believed to have absorbed an attack in your stead. In the same vein, if your Jade becomes cloudy or dull, it is thought to have absorbed negative energy meant for you.

## WHAT CAN JADE DO FOR YOU?

Jade encourages you to live a prosperous life. To be prosperous is to be successful in all areas of your life—from your work to your health to your overall happiness. Jade propels you to thrive in each of these areas.

Jade's lush green color represents nature and its renewing cycle of abundance. Jade is a stone of longevity—it isn't a quick fix, but rather a tool for long-term planning. With a "plan-ahead" mentality, you will be on the path to overflowing success. This stone helps you to achieve your goals and attract new opportunities—both of which lead you toward prosperity.

Think of Jade as your trusted companion, urging you to make wise decisions. When you work with Jade, you are tapping into an ancient dynasty of wisdom. Connect with this wisdom to learn what prosperity means to you and which actions to take in order to achieve the kind of wealth you want in your life. Jade can help by reminding you to make choices now that will allow you to reach the levels of prosperity you are looking for in the future. Whether it's a flourishing love life, thriving health, or financial success, Jade has you covered.

Jade not only empowers you to make smart decisions, but it also infuses your life with good fortune, often in the form of new opportunities. Take note if you meet someone out of the blue or an unexpected job is offered. Jade encourages you to be open to chance events that boost your ability to be prosperous. With Jade supporting all areas of your life, you've got the perfect recipe for prosperity.

If you feel your path to prosperity is blocked, use Jade to clear the way. Do you have trouble following through with your plans? Do you give up as soon as you encounter bumps in the road? Do you set unrealistic goals and fail to meet them? Let Jade help you overcome self-limiting behavior so you can reach a state of prosperity.

# I am prosperous.

1   Hold your Jade in your hand and say out loud, "I am prosperous," 8 times.

2   Wear a piece of Jade jewelry or carry a piece of Jade with you in your pocket or purse every day.

3   Allow the energy of Jade to infuse prosperity into all areas of your life. Whenever you need a boost of prosperous energy throughout the day, touch your necklace or give your stone a little squeeze.

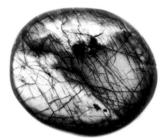

# labradorite

## unleashing your limitless potential

WHEN TO USE IT

When you want to dream big and push past self-limiting beliefs

ORIGIN

Found in Canada, Madagascar, Mexico,
Russia, and the United States

COLOR

Dark gray, with flashes of neon blue,
green, yellow, purple, and pink

## HISTORY & LORE

Labradorite gets its name from the peninsula of Labrador, Canada, where the stone was discovered. It only takes one look at Labradorite's flashy iridescence to understand where the many native legends about this stone come from. According to the lore of First Nations communities in Canada, Labradorite is said to contain the Northern Lights, known as the Aurora Borealis. In the myth, it is believed that the lights were "set free" by one of their ancestors who broke through the rocks with his spear. The lights that remained were set into stone, and thus Labradorite was born.

Labradorite's most renowned quality is known as *labradorescence*. This is what makes the stone transform from a bluish gray to a show of neon illuminations in light.

## WHAT CAN LABRADORITE DO FOR YOU?

Labradorite calls on you to embrace your limitless potential. Living up to your potential means striving to reach your fullest possibilities. With Labradorite, you can go even further. You can go beyond what is expected of you. There is no "I can't" with this stone. Connecting with Labradorite encourages you to believe in the nearly impossible—and then get out of your own way so you can make it happen.

At first glance, Labradorite appears to be a plain dark stone, but a closer look reveals flashes of neon called *labradorescence*. Labradorite's otherworldly energy works its magic on you in the same unexpected way. This stone implores you to seek the light and magic even in the darkest of moments.

Let Labradorite help you tap into a higher state of consciousness and to think *big*. As a stone of destiny and transformation, Labradorite compels you to recognize your strengths in ways you had previously underestimated. By directing your focus toward your future potential, it keeps you from concentrating on your earlier setbacks. If being afraid of disappointment or failure prevents you from striving toward bigger goals, Labradorite can help. Its flashes of light help clear away the self-limiting beliefs and disillusionment that block your inner light from shining through. This stone encourages you to push on, reminding you that there is no limit to your achievements.

When the challenges you've experienced have left you feeling incapable, use Labradorite to reignite your potential. Connecting with this crystal will stimulate both your mental and spiritual power so you can take advantage of the possibilities that surround you. Labradorite allows you to see the world as being full of opportunity rather than adversity. Working with it expands your mind so you can see the magic in the universe and within yourself. When you're ready to dream big and live even *bigger*, let Labradorite illuminate your true, limitless potential!

CRYSTAL INTENTION

# I am limitless.

◇

CRYSTAL PRACTICE

1 Hold your Labradorite in your non-writing hand and say out loud, "I am limitless," 3 times.

2 Still holding your crystal, think of one ambitious goal you would like to bring to life.

3 Hold your crystal and rotate it around in your hand, observing the dimension and flashes of color. Ask yourself, *How can I take action to make my goal a reality?*

4 Continue interacting with your crystal until you receive an image of your goal.

5 Place your Labradorite in a spot where you will see it daily. Every time you catch the flash of your crystal, remember to embrace your limitless potential.

# lapis lazuli

## taking lead in your own life

WHEN TO USE IT

When you want to take charge of your life

ORIGIN

Found in Afghanistan, Argentina, Chile,
Italy, Russia, and the United States

COLOR

Light to dark blue

## HISTORY & LORE

*Lapis Lazuli* translates to "blue stone." This intensely blue crystal has an endless list of associations with legends, royalty, and deities from cultures all over the world. Ancient Chinese and Greek civilizations adored Lapis Lazuli carvings. The stone was even ground and used to create blue paint during the Renaissance, though it was highly expensive.

Ground into powdered form, Lapis Lazuli was also used to create blue eyeshadow in ancient Egypt. Lapis Lazuli was traditionally used in burial ornaments for royalty because of its value, rarity, and healing powers. The famous gold sarcophagus of King Tut was decorated with Lapis Lazuli stones, including around the eyes to represent the blue eyeshadow he would wear. The stone was believed to help lead souls into the afterlife.

## WHAT CAN LAPIS LAZULI DO FOR YOU?

Lapis Lazuli urges you to take the lead. It can be comforting, even relieving, to allow others to make decisions for you. This way, if the choices don't work out the way you intended, you can place the blame on someone else. Instead of relying on others to make a decision for you, let Lapis Lazuli empower you to follow your own lead. You know what is best for you. If you feel like you are allowing your life to be directed by others, Lapis Lazuli will help you step into the driver's seat.

Working with Lapis Lazuli instills the motivation and self-assurance you need to empower your own sense of direction. The deep blue hues of Lapis Lazuli welcome you to experience its deep well of wisdom and recognize the power of your own wisdom. Through recognizing your inner wisdom, you will come to realize that you already have the answers within you. You already know what you want and where you want to go in life. As a stone of truth, Lapis Lazuli ensures that you make choices and decisions in your life in an authentic way that stays true to who you are. This crystal enhances your self-awareness and supports you in taking action toward your own unique path and purpose. Lapis Lazuli empowers you to make life choices with bold conviction.

Lapis Lazuli helps you to realize your authority over your own life. If you find yourself looking to others for permission to switch careers, Lapis Lazuli can help you look no further than yourself. If you feel pressured by society to get married or have children, let Lapis Lazuli remind you that you are in charge of creating your own life. Lapis Lazuli can empower you to trust yourself and live the life you choose.

# I take the lead in my life.

1   Hold your Lapis Lazuli in your non-writing hand and ask yourself, *How can I take the lead in my life?*

2   Still holding your crystal, write down 5 things you can do today to be a leader in your own life. This will be your action plan.

3   Say out loud, "I take the lead in my own life," 3 times.

4   Place Lapis Lazuli on top of your action plan and keep it in your living room, office, or somewhere you will see it every day as you move forward with the steps you've outlined.

# lemurian
# quartz

practicing patience

WHEN TO USE IT

When you feel impatient

ORIGIN

Found in Brazil

COLOR

Clear with a slightly peach tint

## HISTORY & LORE

The ladder-like striations that ascend the facets of the Lemurian Quartz have inspired many questions. This crystal was discovered in Brazil in 1999, but has also been said to hail from a lost Lemurian civilization. Lemuria was believed to have been a continent situated in the Pacific Ocean, described as a tropical civilization full of highly evolved and peaceful citizens.

Lemuria's existence is said to have been focused on wholeness and spirituality. Some believe that these highly evolved beings stored their wisdom inside Lemurian Quartz, which could be unlocked by rubbing the stone. The striations are thought to be programmed by a code that, if unlocked, could bring us into a new reality.

## WHAT CAN LEMURIAN QUARTZ DO FOR YOU?

Lemurian Quartz gives you patience. Instead of anxiously waiting for life to unfold, Lemurian Quartz can help you practice waiting patiently. It can help lessen the burden of urgency, allowing you to take a step back, breathe, and let life unfold in its own time.

The soft energy of Lemurian Quartz helps to quiet the mind of noises and naggings that demand for you to rush without reason. If you're irritated by how long something is taking or how little is being done, this stone can help to quell your frustration. Lemurian Quartz can be extremely beneficial to have on hand during traffic, in airports, and in all other situations that require patience. When faced with a delay or difficulty, it almost always ends better with a touch of patience.

Lemurian Quartz helps you expand your patience by challenging you to accept the fact that there are external factors you cannot control. It invites a sense of peaceful contemplation wherein you can accept the situation at hand and shift your attitude. From this enlightened state, Lemurian Quartz opens the door to the virtues of patience, where you learn to *enjoy* the pause.

If you want it all—love, health, and career—becoming more patient needs to be part of the plan. Lemurian Quartz helps you to reframe situations with a higher sense of acceptance. Trust that you will reach your goals in your own time. Until then, enjoy the process.

Lemurian Quartz reminds you that you have the innate ability to recalibrate yourself, starting with patience. When you have more patience for yourself, your loved ones, and others you meet along the way, you can more fully enjoy life—even the parts that take a little longer to unfold. Let the treasure trove of wisdom in this stone help you to find a deeper patience within yourself.

# I practice patience.

1  Hold your Lemurian Quartz in your hand and say to yourself, *I practice patience*, 3 times.

2  Run your thumb up and down the striations as you take 10 deep, slow breaths.

3  Carry your Lemurian Quartz with you in your purse or pocket to hold on to for times when your patience is tested throughout the day.

# lepidolite

managing anxiety

WHEN TO USE IT

When you feel anxious or nervous

ORIGIN

Found in Australia, Brazil, Canada, Czech Republic,
Japan, Russia, Sweden, and the United States

COLOR

Ranges from light purple to yellow, colorless, or gray

## HISTORY & LORE

Lepidolite's name comes from the Greek translation of "scale," which is a reference to its scaly appearance. It wasn't discovered until 1796 and was initially called Lilalite due to its lavender hue. It is an abundant mineral, with many varieties containing high concentrations of lithium. Lithium, an extremely light metal, has many high-tech uses. Its compounds are even used in some medications to regulate mood disorders.

Lepidolite is also a rich source of other rare elements, including cesium and rubidium. Because Lepidolite contains so many valuable elements, it is highly sought after and mined for extraction. Lepidolite's chemical composition is the reason why it is a prized mineral in metaphysical circles.

## WHAT CAN LEPIDOLITE DO FOR YOU?

Lepidolite helps you manage anxiety. Do you often feel nervous or worried? Does your heart beat rapidly or your breath shorten? Do you have trouble concentrating? These can all be signs of anxiety. Rather than letting anxiety interfere with your life, Lepidolite can help to prevent an escalation. This crystal naturally contains lithium, which is used in antianxiety medication and is known to rebalance emotions. Keep your Lepidolite close whenever you feel anxiety start to get out of control so you can manage it before it's too late.

Lepidolite's soothing lavender color brings calm in times of chaos. Its gentle energy helps to dissolve negativity and ease your mind. Lepidolite is a stone of tranquility that will guide you away from worry and stress and move you toward a state of relief and serenity. Agonizing over future possibilities detracts you from the present moment. Lepidolite reminds you of where you are *now* so your thoughts cannot spiral out of control. It helps you to become conscious of smaller worries and anxieties so you can address them quickly and move on. By recognizing anxious patterns and replacing them with restorative ones, Lepidolite works as a trusted reminder to remain present and calm.

The reassuring energies of this crystal work especially well to comfort you in the heat of the moment, and then guide you to a calmer state of being. Anxiety can be gripping, but working with the energy of Lepidolite will help to release you from its control. Keep Lepidolite close to manage the onset of anxiety before it gets the best of you.

# I let go of my anxiety.

1   Hold your Lepidolite in your dominant hand and say out loud, "I let go of my anxiety," 3 times.

2   Still holding your crystal, begin this breath pattern: inhale for 5 seconds, hold for 5, and then exhale for 5.

3   Repeat this breathing for 1 minute. (If a minute is not enough, continue this breathing until your anxiety passes.)

# malachite

## transforming your life

WHEN TO USE IT

When you're ready for a change

ORIGIN

Found in Australia, the Democratic Republic of the Congo,
France, Morocco, Russia, and the United States

COLOR

Vibrant green with bands and stripes

## HISTORY & LORE

Malachite was a prominent stone in ancient times. Egyptian pharaohs lined their headdresses with the green stone. Ancient Egyptians also ground the stone into a fine powder to create a green pigment. This green pigment was used to create eyeshadow, as well as paint for murals. In ancient Rome, it was believed that Malachite was connected to Venus, the goddess of love. Ancient Chinese dynasties prized Malachite decorative pieces, and Korean dynasties used Malachite powder as paint.

Besides being used for aesthetic purposes, Malachite was used as a healing stone. According to German lore, it was said that wearing Malachite offered protection from danger and could even warn of disasters to come.

## WHAT CAN MALACHITE DO FOR YOU?

Malachite helps you transform your life. Rather than hide behind comfort and consistency, Malachite helps you shake off the behaviors that are keeping you from evolving into the highest version of yourself.

If you are longing for change, Malachite is here to guide you. As one of the most powerful transformational crystals for the heart, Malachite helps bring awareness to that which no longer serves you. Take a hard look at your life—everything from your romantic involvements to your professional endeavors. Malachite can help you pinpoint the areas of your life that are ripe for transformation and then guide you toward transforming them.

Once you are emotionally prepared, Malachite opens your heart to start making the necessary changes to spark a transformation. It guides you toward the kind of unfiltered life advice that you would expect from one of your closest friends, encouraging you to leave behind negative patterns and empowering you to make conscious shifts toward a new and improved way of living.

Malachite makes you aware of the innate transformational energy that has been inside you all along. It helps you grow and evolve in all areas of your life by helping you change your patterns. Do you always seem to go for the same type of partner? Do you tend to stay stuck in a relationship, even when it's clear it isn't going anywhere? Do you and your partner keep breaking up and getting back together? If you find yourself in an unhealthy relationship with relationships, Malachite can help you clear away the patterns of behavior that are holding you back and make room for positive action. Malachite can also shift the way you relate to money. Do you continually spend more than you have? Are you spending what you should be saving for the future? Use Malachite to break free of these cycles and move forward with a healthier financial state. With an intention of transformation and a Malachite crystal, you can take any area of your life and elevate it to a higher state.

# I transform _____.

*(Fill in the blank with an area of your life you want to transform.)*

1 Hold your Malachite in your non-dominant hand and begin observing the patterns and movement in your crystal. Look at the different patterns within the stone. Using it as a visual, ask yourself, *What areas of my life do I need to shift and transform?*

2 Still holding your crystal, choose one area of your life to focus on. Determine one pattern, habit, or belief system you can shift in your life to ignite your transformation.

3 Say out loud, "I transform _____."
*(Fill in the blank with the area you want to transform.)*
Repeat 8 more times.

4 During this time of transformation, carry your Malachite with you in your pocket or purse as a touchstone.

# moonstone

discovering your life purpose

WHEN TO USE IT

When you feel as if you lack direction or purpose

ORIGIN

Found in Australia, Brazil, Burma, India, Madagascar,
Mexico, Sri Lanka, the United States, and many other places

COLOR

Opalescent ranging from colorless to milky white

## HISTORY & LORE

It's not hard to understand how Moonstone, a white luminescent crystal, got its name. Ancient Hindu lore held that Moonstone held trapped moonbeams. In ancient Rome, it was thought that Moonstone received its pearly luster from the stored light of the Moon. The ancient Greeks combined the names of the Moon goddess, Selene, and the love goddess, Aphrodite, and called this crystal Aphroselene.

Moonstone became known as the "Traveler's Stone" due to travelers' belief that Moonstone would protect them and help light their path. However, Moonstone isn't just good luck for travelers—it is believed to be a stone of good luck for all. Its brilliant glow even led to legends that sucking Moonstone could reveal one's destiny.

## WHAT CAN MOONSTONE DO FOR YOU?

Moonstone keeps you on the path toward your life purpose. Have you ever questioned your purpose? Have you ever wondered if you were living the way you were meant to? When you're feeling lost or unsure of which path to take, connect with Moonstone to help you uncover your life purpose so you can bring it to fruition.

This stone holds the divine energy of the Moon, which nourishes your soul and illuminates your purpose. Moonstone helps you get to know yourself on a deeper level and helps you tap into a knowing force from within so you can learn more about what you want your life to be. Once you've become more in tune with yourself, Moonstone opens you up to receive guidance from all around you. As you move through your life, keep your eyes wide open and pay attention to the signs. From a stranger you meet to a chance opportunity, Moonstone makes you more aware of the ways in which life events and encounters can bring you closer to your life purpose.

Moonstone can guide you to make subtle choices to align you with your newfound understanding. Is there a career that you want to explore? A passion that you've pushed off? Moonstone can help you hear the answer and encourage you to follow your life's calling.

If you begin to question your path, Moonstone can offer you the confidence you need to stay the course. Just like the many phases of the Moon, some parts of your journey may feel darker, while other parts will seem brighter. Let Moonstone remind you that there are no wrong turns, and the darker phases are just as important as the lighter ones. Should you feel you've veered off course, work with Moonstone to point you back in the right direction and reconnect you to your purpose. This crystal is here to teach you that sometimes life's greatest twists and turns are lessons in disguise, setting you up to navigate situations that have yet to come.

# I live my life purpose.

1   At night, stand outside under the light of the Moon with your Moonstone.

2   Close your eyes, hold your Moonstone in your hand, and say out loud, "I live my life purpose," 3 times.

3   Open your hands and let your Moonstone soak up the moonlight for a few minutes. Connecting with the energy of the Moon's radiance will give you time to reflect on your life purpose.

4   Place your Moonstone on a windowsill as a reminder to ask yourself, *Am I living a life with purpose?*

# ocean jasper

## prioritizing yourself

**WHEN TO USE IT**

When you're not making time for yourself and your needs

**ORIGIN**

Found in Madagascar

**COLOR**

Varies from blue to green, gray, pink,
and orange, with orb-like patterns

148

## HISTORY & LORE

Most of the history associated with Ocean Jasper is still a mystery to this day. Much of what we do know about Ocean Jasper dates back to the 1990s, when it was found on a beach. This stone has unique spherical patterning that looks like a tie dye of orbs splattered across the stone's surface. At the present time, there have been four distinct Ocean Jasper patterns found. One of the most popular patterns, which features colorful orange and pink orbs, is now extremely rare.

Ocean Jasper is formed through the precipitation of a mineral called silica. When lava cools over the silica, it creates the small spheres that are signature to Ocean Jasper.

## WHAT CAN OCEAN JASPER DO FOR YOU?

Ocean Jasper reminds you to prioritize yourself. Why is it that on your list of things you absolutely *have* to do, nurturing yourself is always at the bottom? Prioritizing some time to rejuvenate your energy isn't selfish or indulgent, it's necessary! If you have trouble setting aside time for yourself and making your needs a priority, connect with Ocean Jasper. The supportive energy of this stone reminds you that your needs are important and helps you learn to prioritize yourself.

Ocean Jasper is also called Cellular Jasper because it is said to reprogram your mind, body, and spirit on a cellular level so you can embrace a calmer, more positive state. Ocean Jasper emits both volcanic and oceanic frequencies. While the volcanic energy reignites the fire within you, the oceanic energy reminds you that it's important to allow soothing energy to flow in as well. Connecting with Ocean Jasper teaches you to take a pause and make space for your needs to be met. It beckons you to put yourself first for a few moments and give yourself the opportunity to soothe your soul so you can return to that fiery and energized state of being.

Just as every Ocean Jasper stone is uniquely decorated, how you prioritize yourself differs from person to person. However you do it, it's important that you make your well-being a priority each and every day. Maybe you carve out 30 minutes to work out or cancel your dinner plans so you can stay at home and rest. Even on the busiest days, you can find 5 minutes to nurture yourself. It doesn't have to be fancy; it just has to be a moment for *you*. Whether you give yourself a moment to sit quietly or you press "snooze" on your alarm for an extra few minutes, call on Ocean Jasper to help you honor yourself today.

# I am a priority.

1   Hold your Ocean Jasper in your hand and say out loud, "I am a priority," 3 times.

2   Sit quietly with your crystal and rub it in your hands. Ask yourself, *What's one thing I can do today to prioritize myself? How can I create time and space to make myself a priority?*

3   Follow through with that act today.

4   Carry your Ocean Jasper with you in your pocket or purse as a reminder to make yourself a priority every day.

# phantom
# quartz

### breaking through blocks

WHEN TO USE IT

When you feel stuck and can't move forward

ORIGIN

Found in Brazil, the United States, and many other places

COLOR

Clear, colorless, transparent to translucent, can have
various colors due to the different mineral deposits

## HISTORY & LORE

Phantom Quartz owes its unique appearance to secondary crystal growths that form within the bigger crystal Quartz, seemingly "haunting" it and leading to its name. These secondary growths are either composed of different kinds of minerals or other types of Quartz, such as Amethyst or Rose Quartz. When Clear Quartz is house to a Milky Quartz phantom, it creates an especially haunting yet beautiful combination.

Phantom Quartz forms when a crystal's growth is stunted or paused due to a block or other environmental cause and a layer of minerals begins to build up. Hundreds or even thousands of years later, the crystal begins growing again and the deposit becomes enveloped by the crystal. The result is the appearance of minerals or crystals floating within the primary Quartz.

## WHAT CAN PHANTOM QUARTZ DO FOR YOU?

Phantom Quartz helps you have a breakthrough. This stone helps you to overcome whatever it is that is blocking your way toward what you want. Whether you're looking to improve your finances, your career, your health, your relationships, or your mindset, Phantom Quartz can assist you. It can help you reach the next level in any area of your life.

Breakthroughs are the result of rising up to meet a challenge. Take one look at Phantom Quartz and you can see this phenomenon frozen in time. As a crystal of growth, Phantom Quartz is all about moving forward. It focuses your mind to search for solutions that will take you where you want to go. When you feel like you've hit a wall, it empowers you to find a new way through. Phantom Quartz will inspire inner growth, inventiveness, and a motivation to succeed within you.

This crystal also sets you up emotionally and mentally for big breakthroughs. Working with Phantom Quartz can be the support system you need. Its calm energy works to quell fears, offering you the perfect space to visualize yourself achieving your goals. While holding on to your Phantom Quartz, ask yourself, *What is one thing in my life that I want to take to the next level?* Is it your relationship? Your finances? Your health? Your career? Your personal or spiritual journey? Program your Phantom Quartz crystal to hold your intention and get ready for a breakthrough.

# My breakthrough starts today.

◇

1    Look at your Phantom Quartz and ask yourself, *In what area of my life do I need a breakthrough?*

2    After choosing an area, write down on one piece of paper any old beliefs, thoughts, or conditioning that you are ready to let go of in that area of your life.

3    After you're finished, rip up your paper and throw it away. Pick up your crystal, hold it in your hands, and say out loud, "My breakthrough starts today."

4    On a second piece of paper, write, "My breakthrough in

_____ starts today."

*(State the area, e.g., my love life, my finances, etc.)*

5    Write out the steps you need to take to make this breakthrough happen.

6    Place your Phantom Quartz on top of your action plan in your bedroom, where you will see it every day. This visual will serve as a reminder to keep moving toward your breakthrough.

# pink opal

having empathy

WHEN TO USE IT

When you lack empathy or are being too self-critical

ORIGIN

Found in Australia, Ethiopia, India, Mexico,
New Zealand, Slovakia, and the United States

COLOR

Pink, with an opalescent shimmer

## HISTORY & LORE

Opal gets its name from the Sanskrit word for "precious stone." Cultures across the world have different histories with Opal. Arabic legends say Opal fell from the heavens in flashes of lightning. Ancient Greeks thought Opals were the solidified tears of Zeus. In India, Opals were believed to be the Rainbow Goddess turned into stone.

Opal was used for a variety of purposes in different parts of the world. It is believed that the crown of the Roman emperor Constantine was embellished with Opal to protect his life and his rule. Australian legend says that the stars were governed by a huge Opal that served as a guide for finding love. Opal was also used as a promise stone in Japanese betrothal jewelry.

## WHAT CAN PINK OPAL DO FOR YOU?

Pink Opal allows you to be more empathetic. Empathy is a two-part process. It requires you to both understand someone else's feelings and to share in them. When you're feeling a lack of empathy, connect with the energy of Pink Opal.

Pink Opal shifts the focus from yourself to another so you can learn to acknowledge someone else's struggle or difficult situation. Pink Opal helps to balance your own emotions so you can approach someone in need with a calm and centered demeanor. This stone opens your heart to feeling what others feel, without judgment. It lends an attitude of compassion and love that helps you find common ground with everyone you encounter. By creating space in your heart to share in others' experiences, connecting with this crystal also enhances your ability to truly feel what others feel.

As an added benefit of working with Pink Opal to practice empathy toward others, you will learn to be more empathetic with yourself. Self-empathy is a powerful tool for developing a positive and loving relationship with yourself. If this seems difficult for you, Pink Opal can help.

If you routinely find yourself sticking to one perspective without allowing for empathy, it's time to work with Pink Opal. This crystal encourages important growth within your spirit. Next time you notice yourself judging someone else's behavior, Pink Opal will inspire you to take a moment to truly see and hear the situation from their point of view. When you're ready to let love, compassion, and understanding inspire you, Pink Opal will establish a deeper sense of empathy.

# I am empathetic.

1  24 hours after an argument or disagreement, hold your Pink Opal in your hand and say out loud, "I am empathetic," 3 times.

2  While still holding your Pink Opal, reflect on the situation. Put yourself in the other person's shoes. Squeeze your Pink Opal and visualize the situation through the other person's eyes. Ask yourself, *How could I have been more empathetic?*

3  If you are able to, circle back with that person and share with them your understanding of their point of view. If you are unable to, the next time you find yourself in a similar situation, remember this practice of empathy to see the situation from someone else's point of view.

# pyrite

attracting wealth

When you want to bring more money into your life

ORIGIN

Found in Brazil, Canada, France, Greece, Italy, Japan,
Norway, Peru, Portugal, Spain, and the United States

COLOR

Gold

## HISTORY & LORE

Pyrite gets its name from the Greek translation of "fire" because the stone can be used to create a spark when struck with iron. That's why Pyrite was used in wheel-lock guns to ignite the gunpowder.

In the Middle Ages, alchemists believed that gold was hidden in Pyrite. Pyrite has been discovered in ancient burial mounds. Southwestern Native American tribes used polished Pyrite as a mirror.

Pyrite's nickname "Fool's Gold" comes from its similarity to gold. During the California gold rush, Pyrite dashed the hopes of many forty-niners who believed they'd struck gold, only to find out they'd filled their sacks with Pyrite. Even John Smith—yes, the same one known from Pocahontas—was fooled by Pyrite. He wrote a frustrated letter in which he referred to the stone as "gilded dirt."

## WHAT CAN PYRITE DO FOR YOU?

Pyrite helps you attract wealth. It helps you to radiate with the golden energy of wealth. Pyrite encourages you to see your own worth so you can manifest more money into your life. Its flashy energy can show you how to become a money magnet.

By illuminating financial possibilities, Pyrite ushers you toward a wealthier future. It empowers you to expect more from yourself and the world around you by reminding you of your own worth. If it's time to start making the kind of money you think you deserve, Pyrite can help you shift your perspective. This stone shines a light on the positive opportunities you might not have noticed before, helping to attract new opportunities and energizing you to take full advantage of them. It helps to dissolve self-limiting beliefs and expectations and illuminate your rich potential. By rooting you in your power, Pyrite encourages you to be confident and focused so you are better able to create the wealth you desire.

Pyrite can be used like a financial advisor, nudging you to get clear about your financial goals so you can focus on manifesting them. Money may not always arrive in the form of a paycheck—it can come in unexpected ways as well. Maybe it's a gift or a rebate. Perhaps you receive a bonus at work. Or maybe you find a new passion project that will end up as a moneymaker. Watch for new financial opportunities whenever Pyrite is near. Infused with the willpower and motivation that Pyrite can inspire within you, you will be unstoppable in your pursuit of wealth.

# I am a money magnet.

◇

1  Hold your Pyrite in your hands and say out loud, "I am a money magnet," 8 times.

2  Place your Pyrite in your non-writing hand. On a piece of paper, write down 3 specific areas of your life that you want to attract wealth into (e.g., in your business, in your investments, etc.).

3  Place your paper with your Pyrite on top of it on your desk or somewhere prominent in your home where you will see it every day. Every time its golden glimmer catches your eye, be reminded that you *are* a money magnet.

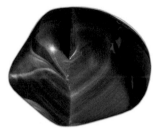

# rainbow
# obsidian

healing from grief

**WHEN TO USE IT**

When you are grieving from a loss, breakup, or separation

**ORIGIN**

Found in Europe, Japan, Mexico, South America,
the United States, and many other places

**COLOR**

Black, with layers of blue, green, red, and pink

---
164

## HISTORY & LORE

Rainbow Obsidian has long been touted for its metaphysical abilities. In the Stone Age, civilizations around the world used Obsidian. Because the rock was easy to break and chip into razor-sharp shapes, it was used to create arrowheads, spears, and cutting tools. Obsidian is still used as a cutting instrument today in some medical devices.

Rainbow Obsidian is formed when volcanic lava cools rapidly. As each layer cools in succession, it creates a rainbow effect within the stone. Most often, the layers within Rainbow Obsidian range through orange, red, pink, blue, purple, and green. Legend says that Rainbow Obsidian is found just after a rainstorm ends and right before a rainbow appears.

## WHAT CAN RAINBOW OBSIDIAN DO FOR YOU?

Rainbow Obsidian helps you heal from grief. Finding comfort and solace with the energy of Rainbow Obsidian can help to ease the trauma of loss. This crystal offers a gentle energy that supports you through the complex emotions of healing.

The energy of Rainbow Obsidian can be an important tool to help you release the pain of loss. There are many things you can grieve over—the loss of a loved one, a marriage, a relationship, a friendship, or a pet, to name a few. You can even grieve over the loss of a job or a previous state of good health. Whatever you are grieving for, Rainbow Obsidian can support you through the process. When you are ready, it will help you begin the journey of healing. Rainbow Obsidian will remind you of your strength and resilience. Use Rainbow Obsidian to work through your pain while allowing yourself compassion and understanding. Rainbow Obsidian, just like you, is stronger than you think.

Keep Rainbow Obsidian close during all the stages of grief, and allow it to absorb your deepest emotions. If you are working through denial, anger, or bargaining, allow this crystal to take on these emotions. Use it as a touchstone for when your emotions begin to get out of hand. If you are feeling depressed, use this stone to remind you that depression is also a part of the process of healing. With Rainbow Obsidian, you can move through the different stages of grief and come out on the other side, where you will eventually find the beginnings of acceptance.

Think of the rainbow colors within this black stone as the light at the end of the tunnel. These colors offer the comfort of knowing you can get through the darkness of your grief. Hand your solemn emotions over to this stone when you are ready to release them. This crystal has a uniquely uplifting quality to it that, when you feel up to it, can help you gather your strength to begin again. When working with Rainbow Obsidian, the heaviness in your heart will grow lighter with each passing day.

# I let go of the heaviness in my heart.

1   Lie down on your back and place your Rainbow Obsidian over your heart for 5 to 11 minutes.

2   As you lie there, say out loud, "I let go of the heaviness in my heart."

3   Allow yourself to cry, get angry, or release whatever emotions come to the surface. Visualize the Rainbow Obsidian absorbing all your pain and hurtful emotions. Let them move through you to let them go.

4   Cleanse your Rainbow Obsidian under running water, and then place it in the Sun for 4 hours.

# red jasper

## stopping procrastination

WHEN TO USE IT

When you find yourself procrastinating

ORIGIN

Found in Brazil, France, Germany, Russia,
the United States, and many other places

COLOR

Red

## HISTORY & LORE

Jasper comes in many colors. The blood-red hue of a Red Jasper crystal comes from iron impurities. Its coloration contributed to the belief that Red Jasper could affect blood flow. Since the 1500s, this crystal has been believed to aid in conception and creative fervor. Ancient Egyptians carved the stone into protective amulets because they believed Red Jasper could ward off negative spirits. According to Native American legend, Red Jasper is the blood of Mother Earth. It was used to facilitate any and all rebirthing. While Ruby is a prized gemstone, it was Red Jasper that High Priest Aaron was said to have chosen instead as one of the 12 stones of his breastplate.

## WHAT CAN RED JASPER DO FOR YOU?

Red Jasper pushes you to conquer procrastination. In your professional life, procrastination can cause you to lose precious time, miss deadlines, ruin careers, damage reputations, make poor choices, and blow opportunities. In your personal life, procrastinating might prevent you from signing the lease at the apartment you want or submitting your job application, or even delay you in getting dish soap for your house before you run out. By orienting you toward action, Red Jasper steers you away from the procrastinator lifestyle and points you toward a life full of success and reward.

Rather than being paralyzed by inaction and delay, Red Jasper inspires you to take action. With its clear, determined vibrations, this crystal can help you set realistic goals so you can move from start to finish without falling into procrastination. Red Jasper's color signifies urgency and action. Its energized yet grounded frequency helps you to feel more stable and supported so you have the foundation to take action in your life. Red Jasper is especially helpful when it comes to sustaining and supporting you during times of stress. Rather than allowing yourself to adopt an attitude of avoidance when times get tough, Red Jasper will empower you to embrace a positive attitude, giving you the motivation to take action.

Working with Red Jasper gives you an adrenaline rush that leaves you no choice but to *do* something. Let Red Jasper be the kick in the pants that you need to start acting more proactively. The truth is, you are fully capable of achieving your goals and fulfilling your responsibilities. Connect with the energy of Red Jasper to take the first step toward completion. When you find yourself deferring life until tomorrow, Red Jasper is the crystal you need to keep procrastination at bay.

# I take action.

1   Hold your Red Jasper in your hand and think of one thing that you've been putting off.

2   Say out loud, "Today, I get started and take action," 3 times.

3   Complete the task you thought of in step 1 within 24 hours.

# rhodochrosite

increasing your self–worth

**WHEN TO USE IT**

When you lack confidence or self-esteem

**ORIGIN**

Found in Japan, Mexico, Romania,
Russia, South Africa, and the United States

**COLOR**

Typically pink with white bands,
though sometimes it appears gray or brown

## HISTORY & LORE

Rhodochrosite is a soft stone that is easily breakable. Because of the difficulty in carving it, all jewelry, statues, and bowls made from Rhodochrosite are prized valuables. The white bands or striations that are common in most Rhodochrosite stones on the market only occur when the stone forms as a stalactite. Translucent Rhodochrosite is less common and far more sought after.

This stone's name stems from the Greek word *rhodokhros*, meaning "rose colored." The Incas, who referred to it as "Inca Rose," believed that Rhodochrosite was the blood of their former kings and queens. According to Hindu beliefs, Rhodochrosite is associated with the heart chakra. This energy center is linked to peace, decision-making, love, and compassion. Rhodochrosite is sometimes known as the Stone of the Compassionate Heart.

## WHAT CAN RHODOCHROSITE DO FOR YOU?

Rhodochrosite helps you know your worth. Often when you think about your worth, you might think of your accomplishments, education, job, or title. But when you tie your worth to these external factors, you miss out on the true value of who you are. Self-worth is internal. It's your value as a person.

Working with Rhodochrosite will encourage you to stop seeking your value from outside yourself, and start finding it from within. This deep raspberry-pink crystal emits a strong and self-confident vibe. A celebratory energy can be felt when you hold this stone, and what it wants to be celebrating is *you*. Go deeper within the layers of who you are, and you will see your value. Look into this crystal's gorgeous deep layers and understand that this is how you should look at yourself. The striations running through this stone make up its particular beauty, just like how your own attributes make up *your* particular beauty.

Instead of letting low self-esteem lead to self-destructive behaviors, Rhodochrosite empowers you to act according to your value. By working with this stone to increase your self-esteem, you will be able to stand fully in your power. You won't settle. Instead, you will go after what you want because you know you deserve it. You will feel fulfilled because you value yourself and your choices. You are more than the sum of your accomplishments. You are valuable because of who you are. Keeping Rhodochrosite close will remind you that no one can take your sense of self-worth away from you unless you give it to them.

If Rhodochrosite feels anything less than love and confidence coming from you, it challenges you to ask why. What's stopping you from acknowledging your worth? Whatever the answer is, Rhodochrosite helps you work through it so you can embrace self-respect, self-confidence, and self-esteem on the other side.

# I am worth it.

1   Hold your Rhodochrosite over your heart and stand in front of the mirror.

2   Ask yourself, *If I felt worthy, what would I do differently?*

3   As you look yourself in the eyes, say out loud what you would do differently. Take this moment in. Say it, feel it, and *believe* it!

4   Continue to look at yourself in the mirror and say out loud, "I am worth it."

5   Carry your Rhodochrosite in your bra or pocket throughout the day as a reminder of your worth.

# rhodonite

learning to forgive

## HISTORY & LORE

Rhodonite gets its name from the Greek word *rhodon*, meaning "rose." This rosy pink stone was first discovered in the Ural Mountains of Russia in the 1790s. A favorite of Russian czars, Rhodonite became a traditional wedding present for royals. Because of its association with love, it is often referred to as a "rescue stone." Rhodonite is an ideal stone for carving and is often formed into beads and used in jewelry.

Rhodonite gets its interesting appearance from a combination of manganese, calcium, and iron. The manganese oxide creates the black veins that give Rhodonite its signature pattern. Rhodonite of a high quality can be translucent and contain very little manganese. These specimens are extremely rare and sought after by collectors.

## WHAT CAN RHODONITE DO FOR YOU?

Rhodonite encourages you to forgive. Rather than harboring toxic feelings, choose forgiveness as a way to heal yourself. Forgiving doesn't mean condoning or excusing hurtful behavior. It means you are no longer ruled by anger or resentment and that you have made peace with the situation and moved on. Forgiveness is like medicine for the heart—you're doing it for *you*. If you are still holding on to anger, blame, or resentment, Rhodonite shifts your perspective. It helps you feel ready to forgive, and then supports you in taking action. This stone wants you to trust that forgiveness is a gift you offer to yourself by offering it to another.

In the same way that this pink stone has black veins through it, your heart also carries dark emotions within. These darker energies can be old grudges and unprocessed blame. The longer these energies remain, the stronger they grow, until finally they begin to wear you down. Rhodonite can be used to rescue your heart by freeing it of resentment and bitterness. Employ it to help release the heavy energy that you have been storing deep inside. Rhodonite will absorb these dense energies, leaving you free of their toxins and able to move forward without the negative emotions that were holding you back.

Once you've let go of the negative emotions, Rhodonite will transform these feelings into positive ones, such as acceptance, love, and understanding. Its gentle vibrations help you to balance your emotions so you can find true forgiveness.

The next time your partner says something hurtful, or your parent says something critical, or your friend lies to you, Rhodonite can help you remember the importance of forgiveness. Leave the conflict in the past and use forgiveness as a bridge for moving on. Forgiving others is also a great practice for learning to forgive yourself. Are you down on yourself for not getting that job or promotion? Did you say or do something you shouldn't have? Give yourself permission to make peace with what happened and move on.

# I forgive.

◇

1   Hold your Rhodonite over your heart.

2   Visualize the person you want to forgive standing in front of you. This person could even be yourself.

3   Say out loud, "I forgive _____."
    *(Fill in the name.)*
    Repeat 6 more times.

# rose quartz

opening yourself to love

## HISTORY & LORE

There are many legends about Rose Quartz and how it came into existence. According to one, Cupid, the Roman god of desire and affection, was said to have bestowed Rose Quartz upon the Earth as a gift of love, passion, and happiness for all. Another Greek legend tells a more tragic tale. According to this myth, Ares, the Greek god of war, came in the form of a boar to kill Aphrodite's lover, Adonis. In trying to save Adonis, Aphrodite cut herself on a briar bush. As their blood spilled, it came together over a Quartz crystal, staining the stone pink. Zeus took pity on the lovers and restored Adonis to Aphrodite for six months of every year.

Rose Quartz was prized by Egyptians, who made facial masks out of the stone and placed it in tombs. The Assyrians were one of the first groups to use Rose Quartz, crafting jewelry from it.

## WHAT CAN ROSE QUARTZ DO FOR YOU?

Rose Quartz is a love magnet. If your love life has hit the brakes or you're having trouble connecting with someone, Rose Quartz can help. By emitting strong vibrations of love, this crystal fills you with compassion, warmth, and tenderness. It teaches you to radiate love from within because when you send more love out, you receive more love back. It opens your heart to romantic love by dissolving any walls you may have placed around it. Rose Quartz will support you in all your journeys for love.

If your heart is feeling guarded, Rose Quartz will encourage you to address the reason why. Have you become so focused on your work that you've closed yourself off from meeting new people or spending time with loved ones? Have you not yet allowed yourself the time and space to fully recover from a heartbreak? Have you become so accustomed to communicating with someone via the Internet that you've forgotten how to communicate with them in person? Work with Rose Quartz to open your heart to love again. This crystal will lend you the confidence you need to put yourself out there.

If your heart is filled with complicated or negative emotions, Rose Quartz can help to flush them out. Rose Quartz empowers you to heal from heartbreak. It wants you to leave behind negative emotions like jealousy and anger, and replace them with hopeful curiosity and a willingness to search for love again.

After doing the internal work to be open to love, Rose Quartz helps you to infuse more love into your romantic life. It supports you in your efforts to set intentions around love and intimate relationships. Are you looking for a loving, committed partnership? Or are you trying to "keep the love alive" in your current relationship? Whether you want to attract love or expand in love, this stone will allow you to see the world through rose-tinted glasses and recognize all the room for love that you have.

# I open my heart to attract love.

◇

1   Hold your Rose Quartz in your dominant hand and reflect on how you approach love. Ask yourself, *What are some of my behaviors and actions that prevent me from opening up to love? What can I do differently to be more open to love?*

2   Place your crystal over your heart and say out loud, "I open my heart to attract love," 6 times.

3   Carry your Rose Quartz in your bra or pocket as a gentle reminder to stay open to love.

# selenite

cleansing yourself and your space

**WHEN TO USE IT**

When your energy and environment begin to feel heavy or dense

**ORIGIN**

Found in Mexico, Morocco, and the United States

**COLOR**

White

## HISTORY & LORE

Selenite is studied in the Naica mine in Chihuahua, Mexico, home to a magnificent cavern filled with these white crystals. In this mine 300 meters below the surface, Selenite forms in enormous crystals the size of telephone poles or redwood trees. Also knowns as satin spar gypsum, Selenite has shed a light on the origins of life on Earth. Prior to 2004, gypsum was only thought to exist on the planet Earth. However, it was confirmed to also be found on Mars in 2004, which hints at the presence of water on Mars, and thus the possibility of life.

In mythology, Selenite was associated with Selene, the Greek goddess of the Moon. This is also where this crystal gets its name.

## WHAT CAN SELENITE DO FOR YOU?

Selenite clears and cleanses energy. Just as dust builds up on surfaces, energy builds up when it isn't cleansed. When your energetic body and environment need cleansing, reach for Selenite. As the highest vibrational crystal on the planet, Selenite works to raise the vibration of everything that surrounds it.

Selenite is a tool like no other. Its high vibrations neutralize surrounding negative vibrations, effectively canceling them out. Selenite raises your vibration to the frequency of its pure, white light. The dreamy white colors of this soft beautiful stone are most often found in long, wand-like formations. You can actually use Selenite to "draw" an invisible bubble of light around you to keep your energy clear and cleansed.

Think of Selenite as being your "energy soap." Selenite helps to wash any remaining "energetic grime" from your day off yourself. After a difficult day, it can wipe the slate clean again so you are ready for the next. Working with Selenite will leave you feeling rejuvenated and refreshed, so much so that you might even feel as though you've taken an energetic shower. Similar to soap, Selenite is the ideal stone for a daily, light cleaning. It removes the first layer of "energy dirt"—the worries or otherwise heavy energies that accumulate during the day and keep you up at night. Without that energetic congestion, you will feel cleaner and clearer.

Once you are cleansed, it's time to do the same for your surroundings. If Selenite is soap for your energy body, it is an air purifier for the energy of your environment. It purifies the darker, heavier energy and raises the vibration so that there is room for lighter energy to fill the space. This crystal, often referred to as "liquid light," flows positive energy into any room in which it is placed. Put Selenite on your windowsill to purify and cleanse your home at all times.

# I am cleansed.

1  Before you go to sleep, lie on your back and place your Selenite over your chest for 5 to 11 minutes.

2  Say out loud, "I am cleansed," 3 times.

3  Visualize your crystal cleansing you of all the energy that has accumulated throughout your day.

4  Place it next to your bed to continually cleanse your mind, body, spirit, and space.

# shungite

detoxifying your mind, body, and spirit

**WHEN TO USE IT**

When you need a detox

**ORIGIN**

Found only in Karelia, Russia

**COLOR**

Black or silver

## HISTORY & LORE

Shungite has been around for an estimated two billion years, but its healing potential was recognized through the 1996 Nobel Prize-winning research that discovered fullerenes within the stone. Shungite is composed mostly of pure carbon and is the only known natural mineral to contain fullerenes, which are specific molecular formations of carbon that act as powerful, long-lasting antioxidants.

Although this scientific breakthrough happened in more recent years, Shungite has been known to purify water long before compressed charcoal or carbon blocks in water filters were used to do the same. In Russia, the only place where this stone is found, springs that pass over Shungite rocks were turned into natural spas in the time of Peter the Great. It was known then, just as it is now, that Shungite works most powerfully when used in conjunction with water.

## WHAT CAN SHUNGITE DO FOR YOU?

Shungite is the stone of detoxification. Because of the fullerenes within the stone, Shungite is a strong and powerful antioxidant. This crystal works to neutralize toxicities produced by damaging emotions, environmental pollutants, or electromagnetic fields, and serves as a master cleanse for your mind, body, and spirit.

When you're feeling foggy or drained, your overall energy is in need of a Shungite cleanse. This crystal's antioxidant effect will detox your physical body by clearing out free radicals that can come from external sources, such as air pollution and pesticides, or from internal problems, including inflammation. Whatever the source, Shungite neutralizes toxins that are present in the body, leaving you feeling restored and re-energized.

Not only is Shungite a powerful tool for physical detoxification, but it also facilitates an emotional detox. It pulls out old emotions and thoughts, and aids in the release of stress, anger, anxiety, negativity, and many other forms of emotional sludge. By facilitating the release of these negative emotions, this crystal leaves you feeling as if a weight has been lifted off your shoulders.

When you need a digital detox, Shungite and its unique properties will support you. Layers of electronic smog caused by constant electromagnetic bombardment leave a thick film over your aura. This invisible sludge is extremely resistant, but the pure and powerful vibrations of Shungite can help to dissolve it. Shungite acts as a protector and a transformer of electromagnetic energy. It has the ability to absorb and neutralize negative energy, harmful chemicals, and the impact of electromagnetic radiation (EMFs).

Shungite can help to detoxify you from the electromagnetic emissions from your home appliances, cell phones, Wi-Fi hot spots, and computers that surround you daily. Shungite does not interfere with the function of the electronics it protects against. Instead, it absorbs the influence of harmful radiation, effectively removing it from your environment. Shungite can be placed on your phone or by your computer to absorb the EMFs before they get to you. You can also carry Shungite with you in your pocket to absorb EMFs wherever you go.

CRYSTAL INTENTION

## Detoxify me.

CRYSTAL PRACTICE

1   Take a Shungite-infused detoxifying bath or shower. If you are taking a bath, first, make sure the crystals are big enough not to fall down the drain. Then draw your bath and place your Shungite directly in the water. If you don't have a bathtub, hang a mesh bag filled with Shungite over the shower head.

2   Soak in the bath for 10 to 20 minutes or let the Shungite water wash over you for the duration of your shower.

3   While in your bath or shower, say out loud, "Detoxify me."

# smoky quartz

letting go of what no longer serves you

WHEN TO USE IT

When you're dwelling on the past or things that don't serve you

ORIGIN

Found in Australia, Brazil, Madagascar, Scotland,
the United States, and many other places

COLOR

Light to dark smoky gray and brown

## HISTORY & LORE

Smoky Quartz is the national gem of Scotland. In Celtic cultures, Smoky Quartz was sacred to the Druids. This stone represented the dark power of the Earth gods and goddesses. It was also associated with the ancient Greek goddess, Hecate, the goddess of magic.

Smoky Quartz regained popularity during the Victorian era in Britain. It was often worn in mourning jewelry in the 19th century. Mourning jewelry were decorative pieces worn by those who had suffered a loss. Darker stones, like Smoky Quartz, were a staple of these pieces that were often worn for a customary period of one to two years. Queen Victoria began this trend when she wore mourning jewelry after the death of her husband, Prince Albert.

## WHAT CAN SMOKY QUARTZ DO FOR YOU?

Smoky Quartz helps you let go of that which no longer serves you. Just as there is smoke after a fire, there's a cloud of raw emotion after a difficult time in your life. Ruminating in these feelings can lead to holding on to them much longer than is necessary or healthy. If this kind of emotional struggle is keeping you stagnant, it's time to connect with Smoky Quartz. Let Smoky Quartz support you on your journey to release what doesn't serve you and create room for what does.

Smoky Quartz presents itself as a serious and somber stone, and it is. It has one job: to help you let go. The darkness of this stone reminds you that you don't have to carry your darker energies with you. Smoky Quartz works in conjunction with Mother Earth. This crystal nudges you to stop wallowing in self-pity and release your emotional baggage, helping you to move on from painful memories and allow the Earth to take them off your hands.

When you are able to let go of beliefs and behaviors that don't have a positive purpose, you are able to make room for those things that do. Smoky Quartz helps you to clear stale, heavy energy and let in fresh, new energy instead. This stone helps you refill yourself with positivity, joy, and light. Smoky Quartz guides you toward a higher state of being where you have the awareness and clarity to recognize what is productive in your life and what needs to be eliminated.

Are you harboring negative emotions like jealousy, fear, anger, regret, or guilt? Have you been holding on to an old grudge? Are you trying to control things that are out of your control? In a toxic relationship? Going through divorce? A slave to bad habits or addictions? Bound by unhealthy attachments? Saying "yes" to any of these questions means you have some letting go to do. Smoky Quartz can guide you to break free from the shackles of what no longer serves you and move on toward a life filled with light and joy.

# I let go.

1. Hold your Smoky Quartz in your non-writing hand and write down all the things you want to let go of in your life.

2. Read your list. Say out loud, "I let go of _____."
   *(Fill in the blank with the things on your list.)*

3. Visualize your crystal absorbing everything you want to release from your life.

4. After you're done, rip up your list and throw it away.

5. Place your Smoky Quartz in the Sun for 4 hours to cleanse it.

# sodalite

## communicating clearly

**WHEN TO USE IT**

When you need to find your voice, speak up for yourself, or express yourself

**ORIGIN**

Found in Canada, Germany, India, Russia, and the United States

**COLOR**

Deep blue, often with some white veining

## HISTORY & LORE

Sodalite gets its name from the rich sodium content within the stone. It was first discovered in 1811 in Greenland, and it gained popularity as an ornamental stone in 1891 when deposits were found in Ontario, Canada. Because these deposits were discovered at the same time as a visit from the royal family, in Canada Sodalite is sometimes referred to as Princess Blue.

Sodalite is a popular stone for jewelry because it is both abundant and easy to carve. Sodalite is often mistaken for Lapis Lazuli, because of its rich blue tone. As early as 2600 B.C., Sodalite was being traded by the Caral people of Peru as well as by the indigenous people of Tiwanaku in modern-day Bolivia.

## WHAT CAN SODALITE DO FOR YOU?

Sodalite helps you communicate clearly. You've probably heard it before, but communication is key. Not only does clear communication help you to express your truth, it also helps others to understand it. If you have lost the ability to speak up for yourself or you are speaking without being heard, Sodalite can help you reclaim your voice.

When you need to communicate clearly, let Sodalite help. Known as a poet's stone, Sodalite encourages you to express yourself authentically. This deep-blue-and-white-speckled crystal brings a light energy to your words. Its nurturing frequencies will help you speak from your heart instead of your head. Sodalite fills you with trust, acceptance, confidence, and the self-esteem you need to share your wants and needs with others. If communication makes you nervous or uncomfortable, let the calming effect of Sodalite help you communicate with comfort and ease.

Sodalite can work with you to help you find your voice during tough conversations. It puts you in touch with your true self and inspires you to communicate from an authentic, honest, and truthful place. When your words align with your heart, there is little room for misinterpretation. Sodalite brings balance and harmony to your words so you can say what you mean and mean what you say.

Rather than communicating online, where your intentions can be hard to decipher, Sodalite inspires you to take your conversation *off*-line, so you are accurately understood. Rather than shying away from the truth of the matter, Sodalite inspires you to boldly state your needs. Rather than letting fear silence you, Sodalite inspires you to express yourself. It gives you the calm clarity to speak in a respectful manner that others will respond positively to.

When you are having trouble communicating, ask yourself: *Am I consciously communicating? Am I taking responsibility for my feelings? Have I identified what it is that is causing me to be misunderstood? Am I clear about what I want?* Use Sodalite to empower your words and the meanings behind them.

# I communicate clearly.

1   Place your Sodalite over your throat and say out loud, "I communicate clearly," 3 times.

2   Using your cell phone, record what you would say to the intended person.

3   Play back your recording and really listen to your words.

4   Hold your Sodalite in your hands, close your eyes, and visualize how you'd like the conversation to go. Ask yourself: *Is there a better way to express myself? Can I be more clear and direct?*

5   If the answer is yes, take time to reconsider how you can communicate more clearly.

# sunstone

spicing up your sex life

**WHEN TO USE IT**

When you want to spice up your sex life

**ORIGIN**

Found in Canada, India, Norway, Russia, and the United States

**COLOR**

Mostly orange or red and can have hints of brown, gray, and white

## HISTORY & LORE

Until Sunstone was discovered in Norway and Siberia, it was considered a rare stone that was highly desirable and expensive. In the Warner Valley of Oregon, Native Americans had been collecting Sunstone for many years.

According to Native American legend, Sunstone came about from the blood of a great warrior who was wounded by an arrow. The warrior's blood, which gave Sunstone its red color, carried his spirit into the stone. In ancient Greece, Sunstone represented the god of the Sun, Helios (or Apollo).

In Viking culture, Sunstone was seen as a compass capable of lending guiding energy to one's travels. Sunstone was placed on a ship's mast, as well as in some Viking graves, to point voyages and spirits in the right direction.

## WHAT CAN SUNSTONE DO FOR YOU?

Sunstone helps you spice up your sex life. Not only is sex a healthy part of a relationship because it boosts intimacy and connection, it's also *healthy*. It's been linked to heart health, longevity, and stress relief. Bottom line is that you should be having sex—and great sex at that. Work with Sunstone to do just that.

Sunstone inspires creativity in the bedroom. Sexual pleasure requires an attitude of letting go and allowing yourself to be in the moment. If you find it difficult to let go and receive pleasure, Sunstone can help you to relax and remember that sexual intimacy is meant to be enjoyed. It's time to unlearn anything that's holding you back from fully embracing passionate sex. Sunstone's creative forces also encourage you to try new things. Keep the lights on. Initiate sex without planning it ahead of time. Be spontaneous. Try it somewhere *besides* the bedroom. Get creative! The excitement of doing things differently will surely spice up your sex life.

When you want to heat things up in the bedroom, Sunstone is your secret crystal weapon. Because it carries the energy of the Sun, Sunstone is all about heat. Its spicy vibe emits sexuality, reducing your inhibitions and enhancing your sex life. Sunstone is a confidence builder, and with confidence comes enthusiasm and drive. Sunstone will give you the confidence to speak up, to try new things, and to reignite the flame that may have burnt out long ago. The confidence that Sunstone instills will allow you to feel comfortable talking about sex with your partner, and exploring with them what you each want and desire. Combine the confidence, creativity, heat, and passion that Sunstone provides and you have the recipe for great (and safe) sex. Now all you have to do is do it!

# I have great sex.

◇

1   Hold your Sunstone and say out loud, "I have great sex."

2   Rest your Sunstone on your nightstand, on your dresser, or somewhere by your bed.

3   Every time you see your Sunstone, remind yourself to tap into your sensual self!

# tiger's eye

### building courage

**WHEN TO USE IT**

When you want to overcome fear

**ORIGIN**

Found in Australia, Brazil, South Africa,
the United States, and many other places

**COLOR**

Yellow with golden-brown stripes

## HISTORY & LORE

Tiger's Eye is best known for the luminescent, golden bands along its surface that have inspired beliefs and myths for thousands of years. Tiger's Eye has been used for courage by warriors and soldiers since ancient times. Roman soldiers accessorized with Tiger's Eye rings for strength and protection before going into battle. They believed that Tiger's Eye was the best stone for battle because of its eye-like appearance. The eye was believed to be all seeing, which was critical for the battlefront.

Besides warriors and soldiers, other members of ancient civilizations used Tiger's Eye. Ancient Chinese believed that Tiger's Eye brought good fortune to the wearer. Tiger's Eye was connected to the magical tiger, the king of beasts in Eastern mythology, which symbolized courage, integrity, and correct use of power.

## WHAT CAN TIGER'S EYE DO FOR YOU?

Tiger's Eye brings you courage. Being courageous does not mean that you are not afraid. In fact, courageous people find their strength at the intersection of fear and motivation. It is the ability to *act* on fear that separates the courageous from the rest. Tiger's Eye helps you to be more courageous by helping you to move through whatever it is that's holding you back—whether that's fear, doubt, uncertainty, or pain.

Tiger's Eye helps you get centered and calm, regardless of the obstacles ahead. Its motivating energy fills you with the power and confidence you need to pursue even the most challenging paths. It inspires you to step out of your comfort zone and push past self-limiting beliefs. Working with Tiger's Eye helps you confront your fears, doubts, and worries, so you can move forward with your life. This crystal reminds you that you are capable of more than you know.

Being courageous takes mental discipline and hard work, but Tiger's Eye is there to support you along the journey. Having a difficult conversation with a co-worker, moving to a new city, changing careers, and standing up for what's right in the face of criticism are all intimidating situations that require a certain level of courage. Tiger's Eye helps you to shift your perspective so that you are able to embrace these difficult times as opportunities to prove your fearlessness and resilience.

Tiger's Eye begs you to ask yourself if you're up to the challenge. Are you going to live in fear or conquer it? With courage, you can choose to take action regardless of your apprehension. And with Tiger's Eye, you can embody the same courageous spirit that those who you most admire seem to embody. Rather than letting fear stand in your way, let your Tiger's Eye crystal inspire you to act on fear instead of feeling paralyzed by it.

# I am courageous.

1  Hold your Tiger's Eye in your hand and bring to mind the fear you want to overcome.

2  Stand tall with your feet firmly planted on the ground.

3  Place your Tiger's Eye over your heart and say out loud, "I am courageous," 3 times. Say it louder and more powerfully each time.

4  Carry your Tiger's Eye in your pocket to give you courage as you conquer that fear.

# tourmalinated quartz

## shifting negativity

**WHEN TO USE IT**

When you want to shift your mind-set from negative to positive

**ORIGIN**

Found in Brazil

**COLOR**

Clear with embedded black rods

## HISTORY & LORE

Tourmalinated Quartz develops into pillar-like structures. When Black Tourmaline appears in Clear Quartz, the inclusions look like tiny pillars sprinkled within the Clear Quartz crystal.

Black Tourmalinated Quartz is sometimes connected to the Hindu deity Ganesh, remover of obstacles. If you are starting on a new endeavor, you may want to call upon Ganesh. Let Ganesh bless your new venture. According to legend, Ganesh's *vahana* is a mouse. (A vahana is a mystical entity that a deity uses as a vehicle or a mount.) Ganesh is typically found accompanied by a mouse to represent an extension of Ganesh's powers by gnawing through all barriers.

## WHAT CAN TOURMALINATED QUARTZ DO FOR YOU?

Tourmalinated Quartz transforms a negative mind-set into a positive one. Made of Clear Quartz crystal and rods of Black Tourmaline inclusions, Tourmalinated Quartz is the convergence of two stones. The Black Tourmaline within the stone is known for absorbing negative energy and protecting the spirit. The Clear Quartz that surrounds the Black Tourmaline is the ideal crystal for programming intentions. If you want to set an intention to remove your defeatist attitude, Tourmalinated Quartz is the crystal to work with.

By shifting your mind-set from "I can't" to "I can," Tourmalinated Quartz helps you break through obstacles. The more negativity you allow to grow within your mind and spirit, the more it takes over your life. You may become reclusive or miss important opportunities that might have otherwise yielded success. You might stop investing in yourself or stop trusting others. If you find yourself having more negative thoughts than positive ones, Tourmalinated Quartz will help you to pause and reconsider your attitude. This crystal will absorb the negativity you've become accustomed to feeling and help you shift toward positivity instead. Once you begin to feel more positive, Tourmalinated Quartz can act as a gauge, encouraging you to stay on the path of positivity.

Use Tourmalinated Quartz as a visual reminder of what your mind looks like when negativity invades—a clear, blank slate permeated by lines of black, dark thought. The more you are able to bring awareness to the dark thoughts within your mind, the more power you have to transform them into light.

When working to remove negativity from your mental vocabulary, start to notice your most frequent negative thoughts. Do you often find yourself saying things similar to "I can't lose weight," "I can't get a job," "I can't find love," or "I can't quit smoking"? If these are your first thoughts, work with Tourmalinated Quartz and a positive intention to slowly but steadily break down your old mind-set and build toward a new positive one.

# I shift my mind-set from negative to positive.

1 Hold your Tourmalinated Quartz in your dominant hand and gently close your eyes. Bring your negative thought to the forefront of your mind.

2 Still holding your crystal, say out loud, "I shift my mind-set from negative to positive," 3 times.

3 Shift your thought from negative to positive. Reword it completely in your mind!

4 Say your new positive thought out loud 9 times.

# turquoise

## prioritizing your health

### WHEN TO USE IT

When you want to focus on your health

### ORIGIN

Found in Africa, Belgium, China, France, Iran, Mexico, the United States, and many other places

### COLOR

Varies from blue to bluish green

212

## HISTORY & LORE

Adored for centuries, Turquoise rocks have been carved and set into everything from royal thrones and daggers to jewelry and cups. The Egyptians believed Turquoise brought good fortune and made them invulnerable. They carved the stone into symbolic jewelry and statues, such as their scarab pectorals.

Use of Turquoise dates as far back as 5500 B.C., when it was believed to prevent accidents and cure diseases of the head and the heart. One legend suggests that throwing a piece of Turquoise into a river will bring rain.

Turquoise was a sacred stone to many Native Americans. Medicine men used Turquoise in their healing practices. Often carved into the shape of animals, Turquoise was placed in tombs, believed to guard the dead and invite protective spirits.

## WHAT CAN TURQUOISE DO FOR YOU?

Turquoise empowers you to prioritize your health. Often referred to as the master healer stone, this crystal reminds you that health is the most important aspect of your life. If taking care of yourself has fallen to the last item on your to-do list, use Turquoise to bring it back to the top again. This stone gives you the support you need to address your health, both mental and physical.

The healing frequencies of Turquoise will connect you to the energy of the Earth. Mother Nature is in a constant state of renewal, as are you. Heal, renew, regenerate; this is the never-ending cycle of Turquoise energy. The stone's blue hues also connect you with the healing energy of water, the element needed to sustain all life. By combining the Earth energy of renewal and the life-giving energies of water, this crystal carries the ideal energies to support all areas of your health.

Turquoise is a programmable stone, which allows you to set specific healing intentions. Do you want to create a new habit or behavior that promotes a healthy lifestyle? Do you have a specific ailment that you want to conquer? Is your mental health your priority? Use Turquoise to set precise intentions for all types of healing. And once you've set your intention, let Turquoise be your personal trainer, nutritionist, and life coach all in one. It will motivate you to bring your perfect vision of health to reality. Make that appointment you've been putting off. Take the time to eat healthy. Create a regular exercise routine. Try meditation. Find stress-relieving activities. Regardless of where you are in your healing journey, Turquoise empowers you to reclaim your health without fear or hesitation.

Don't know where to begin? Tune in to your body for the answers. Your body has its ways of telling you what it needs . . . are you taking the time to listen? Connect with Turquoise to understand your body's signals so you know exactly what needs to be done to achieve optimum health.

# I am healthy.

1   Hold your Turquoise in your hands and say out loud, "I am healthy," 3 times.

2   Ask yourself, *What's one thing I can do today to focus on my health?* (e.g., making a doctor's appointment you've been putting off; starting an exercise routine; preparing yourself a healthy, homemade meal; etc.). Be as specific as possible.

3   Take action on that one thing today.

# unakite

## cultivating gratitude

WHEN TO USE IT

When you need a reminder to be grateful for all that you have

ORIGIN

Found in Brazil, South Africa, the United States, and many other places

COLOR

Green and pink

## HISTORY & LORE

Unakite was named after the Unaka Mountains of North Carolina, where it was first discovered. It's also been found on the shores of Lake Superior and along rivers in Virginia after being washed down from mountains and glaciers. Unakite is known for its unique appearance, which combines olive green with a sprinkling of pink. While it may look like a marriage of Jade and Rhodochrosite, Unakite is actually composed of a combination of Red Jasper and Epidote, which is why Unakite is sometimes mistakenly identified as Epidote.

Unakite is thought to assist in meditation by encouraging a sense of presence. The durability of this stone has made it useful for architecture. You can find Unakite trimming the front steps of the Smithsonian National Museum of Natural History in Washington, D.C.

## WHAT CAN UNAKITE DO FOR YOU?

Unakite lends an attitude of gratitude. Have you ever shared with a group of friends or family what you are thankful for? That is a very small-scale representation of what it means to practice gratitude. But there is so much more room for gratitude outside of a once-in-a-blue-moon occasion. Unakite will help you tap into a more thankful and appreciative mind-set every single day so you can live a life full of gratitude.

Unakite encourages you to create a practice of gratitude. The reason that it's often referred to as a gratitude "practice" is because shifting toward a more grateful mind-set takes consciousness, awareness, and sometimes a little help. That's where Unakite comes in. Unakite is the stone of "living in the now." It holds a grounding energy that connects you to the present moment, where you can embrace a grateful mind-set for where you are and what you have right now. It reminds you to enjoy the small moments and little things in life.

Gratitude is not just in your head; it also lives in your heart. Unakite connects you to your heart space where you can tap into the loving energy that allows you to remember what you appreciate most. When you come from a place of love, you can focus on those aspects of life that you love and are grateful for. This compassionate, loving, kind, and appreciative energy overpowers any negativity that lives in your head or in your heart so you can purposefully focus on the blessings in your life.

When you have trouble finding those parts of your life that you are grateful for, Unakite will be your constant reminder of all that you have. Are you grateful for your health? Or the family and friends that surround you? Are you grateful for your home, your ability to travel, your job? Maybe it's something even smaller, like a homemade meal. Unakite will fill you with thankfulness for the highlights of your life, big and small.

# I am grateful.

1   Start a gratitude journal. Every night before you go to sleep, hold your Unakite in your non-writing hand, and write down 3 things you are grateful for.

2   Place your Unakite on top of your journal until the next day.

# 30 CRYSTAL COMBINATIONS

Crystals are powerful when worked with individually, but combining crystals can supercharge your intention and take it to the next level. Take love, for example. When you want more love in your life, you have to be open to love, act and speak from a place of love, and let go of patterns that don't serve you. Each facet of your intention requires the energy of a different crystal, and all the energies together have a unified energetic effect.

Combining the energies of different crystals shifts the way you use them since using crystals in combinations can affect each other and highlight different parts of their energy, resulting in a stronger overall energy combination. Although the uses of the crystals may differ slightly from combination to combination, rest assured that they are working together to bring your intention to life.

# being
# patient

Patience is a virtue, but it's also challenging to be patient in a world that moves so fast. Being patient prevents you from snapping, losing your temper, or feeling overwhelmed. Practice patience every day in big or small ways—from waiting in line at the coffee shop to waiting for the job you've been wanting. Use these crystals when you need more patience.

AGATE will help you create balance in your life so you don't feel rushed or overwhelmed. This stone reminds you that preserving boundaries is crucial when maintaining patience. It's easy to lose your patience when you are being pulled in too many directions. Learning to say "no" to people and situations will prevent you from spreading yourself too thin and risking a short temper.

BLUE LACE AGATE encourages peace of mind. Its soothing blue tones support calmness and tranquility, both of which lend patience to a hurried mind. This stone specifically helps you manage your fight-or-flight responses, so you can resist being upset or angry and instead approach the situation at hand with grace and composure.

CELESTITE offers a soothing and calming energy that encourages you to push pause. This crystal allows you to look at a situation from a higher perspective so that you can elevate your state of being, relax, and breathe deeper.

LEMURIAN QUARTZ is your modern-day "worry stone." When you feel impatient, rub your thumb over its natural striations to calm down.

CRYSTAL INTENTION

## I am patient.

CRYSTAL PRACTICE

1   Hold your crystals in both hands and say out loud, "I am patient," 5 times.

2   Place Celestite in your home and at work to remind you to be patient.

3   Carry Agate and Blue Lace Agate in your pocket or purse throughout the day as a reminder to be patient.

4   Keep Lemurian Quartz in your car for times when you become impatient while driving (e.g., traffic, road rage, can't find parking, etc.). Rub your thumb over the striations until you return to a calm state of mind.

# boosting your energy level

When you feel low in energy, it is your body's way of getting your attention. Take steps to boost your energy level so you can go from exhaustion and depletion to restoration and rejuvenation. These crystals can help you make better decisions to heighten your energy level.

BLOODSTONE helps to get your blood pumping by encouraging you to get up and move. It can be hard to convince yourself to get moving when you are feeling fatigued, but it's the best way to refuel your system and get energized.

GARNET reinvigorates your passion for life. When your life becomes monotonous and stagnant, you start to feel depleted. Garnet reminds you to do more of the things you feel passionate about to bring that spark back.

MALACHITE transforms your energy level. It inspires you to make conscious choices that boost your overall energy.

RED JASPER energizes your body and inspires you to take action. It diminishes negative mind chatter and encourages you, letting you know that *you can do it.*

CRYSTAL INTENTION

# I am energized.

CRYSTAL PRACTICE

1  Hold your crystals in your hands and say out loud, "I am energized," 3 times.

2  Grab 2 pieces of paper, a pen, and your crystals. Set your crystals down in front of you and set a timer for 3 minutes.

3  On your first piece of paper, write down everything that leaves you feeling depleted, tired, or drained. After the timer goes off, read what you wrote.

4  Set your timer again for 3 minutes. On your second piece of paper, write down solutions to improve and boost your energy level. Is there a way you can shift your schedule around? Can you go to bed earlier? After the timer goes off, read what you wrote.

5  Circle one thing you can take action on to raise your energy level today.

6  Place your Garnet, Malachite, and Red Jasper in your kitchen. Carry your Bloodstone in your bra or pocket throughout the day to boost your energy level.

# career

Professional life can be both exciting and overwhelming.
Whether you're starting a career or changing careers,
it's essential to know what you want, and then work
hard toward your professional goals. Staying focused,
determined, and passionate will help you to be successful
in all that you do. Use these crystals to support your
career, whatever stage you are in.

AMAZONITE helps you remain hopeful and optimistic about what's next in your professional life. It reframes your perspective with optimism so that you can trust that it will all work out in the end—even when your career path is full of challenges.

AVENTURINE brings luck to your endeavors. Having luck on your side always benefits you in a professional setting, as many times your career can depend on the choices and actions of other people. Aventurine ensures that you catch those lucky breaks.

CARNELIAN helps you to share your talents. This stone gets your creativity going so you can bring your original ideas or creations to the conversation.

CHRYSOCOLLA inspires you to start fresh in the workplace, whether you're new to the workforce or an experienced professional. If you're feeling called to start anew, Chrysocolla will encourage you to take the leap into a new chapter of your career.

CLEAR QUARTZ helps you get clear on what your gifts are and what you want to do for a living.

EPIDOTE helps you heal from betrayal. If you were blindsided by a co-worker or an unexpected termination at work, this stone helps you recover and rebuild trust. It supports you as you move through any toxic feelings of anger, confusion, or hurt by absorbing them and guiding you toward a brighter tomorrow.

GARNET fills you with passion. It gets you excited about your work and your professional experiences. When you exude passion, others will start to notice.

JADE brings prosperity in your career. Working with this stone will help you flourish and thrive in whatever position and industry you choose.

**LAPIS LAZULI** empowers you to take the lead in your career. Do you want to advance your position? Do you want to start a new project or take on more responsibility? This stone encourages you to tap into your wisdom and knowledge so you can get to where you want to go.

**MOONSTONE** connects you to your life purpose. If you realize that you aren't living out your purpose, this stone lends you the support to realign yourself with what you are meant to do.

**PYRITE** helps you identify your financial goals. When you know what kind of wealth you want to cultivate, you can take the necessary steps in your career to make it happen.

**RAINBOW OBSIDIAN** supports you as you move through feelings of grief after the loss of an old job or career. This stone absorbs your grief so you can release any hurt and negative emotions.

**RED JASPER** motivates you to take action in your career. Stop putting off what you want until the timing is better. There's never a more convenient or more perfect time to make a change, so do it now!

**SELENITE** cleanses your mind and body of any toxic thoughts or feelings that arise throughout your career. This stone helps to wipe your emotional and mental state clean and restores you to your brightest self.

**SMOKY QUARTZ** allows you to let go of the past. Stop holding on to anything that no longer serves you, whether it's a negative experience or a toxic mind-set. Let this crystal help you move forward and focus on the possibilities that fill your future.

**SODALITE** gives you the tools to ask for what you want, from a new task or a higher salary. It encourages you to speak up for yourself and be honest with others.

# CHOOSING A CAREER

CHRYSOCOLLA
CLEAR QUARTZ
JADE

### CRYSTAL INTENTION

## I'm ready to start my career.

### CRYSTAL PRACTICE

1   Hold your crystals in your hands and say out loud, "I'm ready to start my career."

2   Put down all of the crystals except Clear Quartz, and get clear on what it is that you want to do.

3   Put down Clear Quartz, pick up Jade in your non-writing hand, and make a list of jobs that are related to your interests.

4   Put down the Jade, pick up Chrysocolla, and connect with it to jump-start your job search. Begin researching companies and available jobs that would be of interest to you. Carry it with you in your pocket or purse daily as a reminder to take daily action toward starting this new career journey.

# INTERVIEWING FOR A NEW JOB

AVENTURINE
CARNELIAN
GARNET

### CRYSTAL INTENTION

## I am confident and passionate about my interview for

_____.

### CRYSTAL PRACTICE

1   Hold your crystals in your hands and say out loud, "I am confident and passionate about my interview for

_____

_____."

*(Fill in the blank with the position and company you are interviewing for.)*

2   Bring Aventurine, Carnelian, and Garnet with you to your interview.

3   While you are waiting or during your interview, squeeze your crystals for an extra dose of confidence and luck.

# ADVANCING YOUR CAREER

## CRYSTAL INTENTION

### I advance my career.

## CRYSTAL PRACTICE

1 Holding Lapis Lazuli in your non-writing hand, make a list of what you can offer to the position. Include your strengths, your ideas, and how you will add value.

2 Hold your Lapis Lazuli, Pyrite, and Sodalite in your hands and say out loud, "I advance my career."

3 Place your crystals on top of your list in your desk or workspace.

4 Carry Sodalite with you in your pocket to remind you to communicate clearly, ask for what you want, and make it happen.

# CHANGING CAREERS

CARNELIAN

MOONSTONE

RED JASPER

## CRYSTAL INTENTION

### I am ready to begin a new career.

## CRYSTAL PRACTICE

1 Hold your crystals in your hands and say out loud, "I am ready to begin a new career."

2 Lie comfortably on your back and place your crystals as follows:

RED JASPER *over your pubic bone.*

CARNELIAN *above your belly button.*

MOONSTONE *on your forehead.*

3 Bring all your fears and worries about changing careers to mind. Ask yourself, *If I were not afraid, what would I be doing? If I were living my purpose, what career would I have? What are my non-negotiables in this new career? What am I willing to compromise?*

4 Once your thoughts have settled, remove your crystals from your body. Then write a list of your biggest takeaways from this conversation with yourself.

5 Place your crystals on your desk or work space as a reminder to take action in pursuit of your new career.

# QUITTING YOUR JOB

SELENITE

SMOKY QUARTZ

SODALITE

### CRYSTAL INTENTION

**I am moving on to a new opportunity.**

### CRYSTAL PRACTICE

1   The night before you plan to quit your job, hold Selenite, Smoky Quartz, and Sodalite in your hands and say out loud, "I am moving on to a new opportunity," 3 times.

2   Holding Sodalite in your dominant hand, visualize your boss in front of you and rehearse what you plan to say. Repeat this as many times as needed.

3   On the day, keep Sodalite in your pocket as a reminder to communicate clearly as you give your notice.

4   After you quit your job, hold Smoky Quartz in your hand and visualize the crystal absorbing any guilt, sadness, or fear, or any other negative emotions that come up.

5   Close your eyes, hold Selenite over your chest, and say out loud, "I am moving on to a new opportunity," 3 times.

6   Sit with your Selenite for 3 to 5 minutes to clear your mind.

# MOVING FORWARD AFTER GETTING FIRED

AMAZONITE

EPIDOTE

RAINBOW OBSIDIAN

### CRYSTAL INTENTION

**I know that I have something to offer. Another job is waiting for me.**

### CRYSTAL PRACTICE

1   Hold Epidote and Rainbow Obsidian in your hands and say out loud, "I know that I have something to offer. Another job is waiting for me," 9 times.

2   Lie on your back, place your crystals over your heart, and let your emotions out. Allow yourself to feel your grief, sadness, betrayal, anger, and fear. Cry, scream, yell—let it all out.

3   Leave your crystals on your body for 5 to 11 minutes.

4   Cleanse your crystals using your favorite method.

5   Carry Amazonite with you daily in your pocket or purse as a reminder to be hopeful and optimistic in your future career endeavors.

6   Repeat steps 1–5 as needed.

# clearing your mind through meditation

Meditation is extremely beneficial for your health and well-being. It helps you to achieve mental clarity and emotional calm. The word *meditation* can be intimidating to some, but at its core, meditation is simply a practice of quieting the mind. You can meditate in a variety of ways—by setting an intention for your meditation, focusing on your breath, or trying to let your thoughts pass by like clouds in the sky. There is no wrong or right way to meditate, and ultimately it is up to you to discover the way that works best for you. Use these crystals to deepen your meditation. They can help to raise your consciousness and awareness, as well as help you achieve a state of quiet calm.

AMETHYST encourages you to connect with your thoughts. This relaxing stone helps you end the chaotic spiral of endless thoughts running through your head and find mental peace. The more you connect with Amethyst, the more in tune with your thoughts you will become and the more control over your mental state you will have.

CLEAR QUARTZ helps you achieve a clear mental state. It allows you to drown out the noise of your mind and your surroundings so you can get silent. In this clear and quiet headspace, you can give yourself a moment of mental calm.

SELENITE works to cleanse your body of any stuck or stagnant energy to raise your vibration. When your energetic body is lighter, you can draw your attention away from physical distractions that prevent you from getting still.

CRYSTAL INTENTION

My mind is calm and clear.

# MORNING MEDITATION

1  Find a quiet space where you feel comfortable and relaxed.

2  Hold your crystals in your hands and say out loud, "My mind is clear and calm," 3 times.

3  Place your Amethyst in your space to keep your space clear, clean, and light.

4  Sit down and place your Selenite in front of you.

5  Holding a piece of Clear Quartz in each hand, close your eyes and quiet your mind, focusing your attention on your breathing.

6  Meditate with your crystals for a minimum of 3 minutes. (Build to meditating longer over time.)

7  When you are ready, open your eyes and put down your crystals.

# EVENING MEDITATION

CRYSTAL PRACTICE

1  Find a quiet space where you feel comfortable and relaxed.

2  Hold your crystals in your hands and say out loud, "My mind, body, and spirit are clear and calm," 3 times.

3  Lie down on your back and place your crystals accordingly:

   CLEAR QUARTZ *in each hand.*

   SELENITE *over your chest.*

   AMETHYST *just above the space in between your eyebrows.*

4  Close your eyes and quiet your mind, focusing your attention on your breathing. Visualize your crystals absorbing any stress or excess energy from your day.

5  Leave your crystals on your body for a minimum of 5 minutes. (Build to meditating longer over time.)

6  When you are ready, open your eyes and remove your crystals.

# connecting with your spiritual practice

Spirituality differs from person to person. For some, it means connecting to a higher, invisible realm, like that of angels and spirit guides. For others, spirituality is about personal growth. However you choose to connect to it, spirituality can help you find a sense of mental awareness and expansiveness that you didn't have before. Use these crystals when you want to connect with your spirit and propel your spiritual journey.

AMETHYST allows you to tap into your intuition from a peaceful state of mind. Tuning in to your intuition helps you listen to the signals from your highest consciousness so you can better align with your true self on a path toward discovering your spirituality.

ANGEL AURA QUARTZ encourages you to bring a lighthearted energy to your spiritual practice to establish a practice that connects best with you. Your spiritual journey is meant to be enjoyed!

ANGELITE reminds you that you are not alone because your angels surround you. Connecting with this crystal helps you become more aware of the angelic realm and opens your eyes to any signals that your angels are sending you.

LABRADORITE urges you to expand past your own perceived limits. When you see its rainbow flash, the abundance of colors reminds you that your possibilities and potential are endless.

# I am committed to deepening my spirituality.

1   Hold your crystals in your hands and say out loud, "I am committed to deepening my spirituality," 3 times.

2   Lie on your back and place your crystals accordingly:

ANGEL AURA QUARTZ *over your heart.*

ANGELITE *over your throat.*

AMETHYST *in the middle of your forehead.*

LABRADORITE *just above your head.*

3   Touch your hand to your Angel Aura Quartz and say out loud, "I am committed to deepening my spirituality."

4   Repeat step 3 with your Angelite, Amethyst, and Labradorite.

5   Close your eyes and leave your crystals on your body for 5 to 11 minutes. Take this time to connect with your spirit.

# coping with depression

When you fall into a depressive state, it can be disabling. You can feel hopeless, lonely, and trapped, so it's helpful to find little ways to uplift your spirit. Use these crystals to help you cope with depression. While crystals can help you manage feelings of depression, we recommend seeking medical assistance if your symptoms persist or you have thoughts of harming yourself.

CITRINE brings sunshine into the darkness of your mind. Happiness can be a difficult mind-set to tap into when you are overcome with depression. Citrine works to raise your vibration and bring you closer to the light and bright energy of happiness.

LEPIDOLITE naturally contains Lithium, which is often used in medications to regulate mood disorders. With its peaceful, gentle energy, this stone works to relieve any anxiety and manage the onset of depression.

SMOKY QUARTZ helps you to let go of the darkness. It allows you to release heavy emotions by handing all dark and dense energy that is being carried over to your crystal.

UNAKITE encourages you to appreciate the more positive aspects of your life. This stone helps brings awareness to the things you have to be grateful for, big or small. Whether it's a delicious meal or a good day, Unakite makes you more aware of the highs and shifts your mind away from the lows.

# I am coping with my depression.

1   Hold your crystals in your hands and say out loud, "I am coping with my depression," 3 times.

2   Start slowly. When you wake up, hold Unakite over your heart and think of one simple thing that you are thankful for.

3   Keep Citrine on a windowsill in your home. Use it as a reminder to let more light into your life.

4   Before you go to sleep each night, place Lepidolite over your forehead to bring peace to your thoughts. Hold Smoky Quartz in your dominant hand to absorb any released energy and emotions so that you do not have to hold on to them anymore.

5   Repeat steps 1–4 daily.

6   Once a week, place your crystals outside for 4 hours to cleanse and recharge.

# cultivating happiness

Happiness is not only a feeling; it's a choice you can make every moment of every day. By choosing to be happy, you can tap into feelings of joy and contentment whenever you want. Stop waiting for certain things in your life to happen in order for you to be happy. Connect with these crystals and choose happiness today, and every day.

———

ANGEL AURA QUARTZ reminds you to be joyful. Just one look at this stone will bring a smile to your face. It encourages you to embrace a light, playful attitude, just like when you were a kid.

AMAZONITE helps you to see that the world is overflowing with hope and possibility. This crystal reminds you to flip from a pessimistic state of mind to a more optimistic one.

APOPHYLLITE encourages you to maintain a positive mind-set. When you train your mind to see the upside in every situation, choosing to be happy begins to come as second nature. This crystal emits a positive vibration to lift your mood and guide you toward the bright side.

CITRINE radiates light all around you to cultivate happiness and joy. This sunny stone cannot hold negative vibrations and reminds you not to either.

# I am happy.

1  Arrange your crystals in a semicircle. Lie on your back with your head near the crystals.

2  Say out loud, "I am happy," 3 times.

3  Close your eyes and take 3 deep breaths.

4  Visualize light radiating from the crystals and entering your body through the crown of your head and traveling all the way down to your toes, filling every cell of your being.

5  Lie with your crystals for 5 to 11 minutes.

6  When you're finished, place your crystals on your windowsill where they will catch the sunlight.

# dealing
# with
# change

Change can be both scary and exciting, intimidating and appealing. Rather than avoiding or resisting change, learn to embrace it. Use these crystals to welcome change, however big or small, in any area of your life.

———

CHRYSOCOLLA helps you to start fresh. Its energy allows you to feel confident and supported as you begin anew and emerge into the new you.

FLUORITE encourages you to see this period of change as a blessing. It reminds you that with change comes the opportunity to wish for what you always wanted.

LABRADORITE illuminates your limitless potential. Seeing the incredible spectrum of color allows you to imagine the infinite possibilities that are waiting for you.

MALACHITE supports your transformation from one state into the next. It reminds you to leave the past and your old self behind as you move forward into the next stage of your life.

PHANTOM QUARTZ helps you break through any self-imposed limitations. This crystal reminds you that change is a necessary part of your journey and breaking through to that next level.

TURQUOISE facilitates healing and supports you during this time of change.

# Change is good.
# This is an opportunity for me to grow.

1   Hold your crystals in your hands and say out loud, "Change is good. This is an opportunity for me to grow," 3 times.

2   On a piece of paper, write down 1 obstacle that is holding you back from moving forward.

3   Fold your paper up and place your Phantom Quartz on top of it.

4   Hold just your Chrysocolla, Labradorite, and Fluorite and ask yourself, *If I had no obstacles in front of me and no limitations for the future, what would I wish for?* And make that wish!

5   When you're finished, place these two crystals on a windowsill.

6   Lie on your back and place these crystals accordingly:

   MALACHITE *over your heart.*

   TURQUOISE *over your throat.*

7   Close your eyes and leave your crystals on your body for 5 to 11 minutes. During this time, visualize your transformation through this period and into the future.

8   Place the Malachite and Turquoise with your Chrysocolla, Labradorite, and Fluorite on the windowsill.

9   After you've overcome your obstacle, rip up your piece of paper and throw it away.

# enhancing your beauty

Beauty comes from within. When your inner beauty shines through you, you glow from the inside out. Instilling a simple daily practice of combining the energy of crystals with the power of affirmations encourages you to celebrate your beauty each and every day. Use these crystals when you want to tap into your inner beauty.

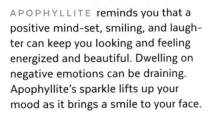

APOPHYLLITE reminds you that a positive mind-set, smiling, and laughter can keep you looking and feeling energized and beautiful. Dwelling on negative emotions can be draining. Apophyllite's sparkle lifts up your mood as it brings a smile to your face.

AQUAMARINE restores inner contentment and encourages self-acceptance. This stone reminds you to embrace yourself fully and lift your spirit up with positive affirmations.

CHRYSOPRASE helps you to connect with your inner beauty and embrace aging gracefully. The beauty that lives within you comes from your wisdom, elevated spirit, inspired living, and loving character. You've earned your beauty, and this crystal reminds you to share it with the world around you.

RHODOCHROSITE encourages you to evaluate whether you are treating yourself as well as you deserve. Are you eating foods that are nourishing? Getting enough sleep? Staying active? When you honor yourself and recognize your worth, you feel good from the inside out.

ROSE QUARTZ reminds you to love all aspects of yourself. When you love and cherish yourself, you radiate and glow with that soft warmth.

# I am beautiful inside and out.

1   Hold your crystals in both hands and say out loud, "I am beautiful, inside and out," 3 times.

2   Begin creating a crystal-infused beauty water. Place your Aquamarine, Apophyllite, Chrysoprase, Rhodochrosite, and Rose Quartz crystals in a glass bowl and cover them with filtered water.

3   Set the bowl in a spot where it can absorb the Sun's energy from sunrise to sunset.

4   After this time period, pour the crystal-infused beauty water into a spray bottle. If your stones fit in your bottle, you can keep them in the bottle as well.

5   Shake well and spritz your face and all around your body every morning as part of your beauty routine.

# fertility &
# pregnancy

The journey to motherhood is exciting and joyful, but it can also be met with worry, fear, and self-doubt. Whether you are trying to get pregnant or are almost ready to give birth, incorporating mindful practices can have an immense impact on your life-giving experience. Connect with these crystals during every stage of your journey to motherhood.

AMETHYST encourages relaxation and peace. It emits a soothing energy to calm your mind, body, and spirit during your pregnancy and while giving birth.

BLACK TOURMALINE protects you and your space during your pregnancy and while giving birth. Connecting with this crystal during childbirth absorbs any fear or chaotic energy in your space, whether it comes from you or those around you.

CARNELIAN connects you with the energy of creating. It helps you to release any energetic blocks that are preventing you from creating new life.

MOONSTONE is associated with the energy of the Moon and the feminine, connecting you with your destiny of motherhood. It is believed to be a stone of fertility and love for women because it helps to unlock the energy of the Moon that resides within you, thereby keeping you in a more balanced state.

PINK OPAL reminds you to be kind and empathetic to yourself throughout your fertility and pregnancy journey. It calms the heart to release feelings of fear and worry and replace them with love and understanding.

RAINBOW OBSIDIAN allows you to bring any feelings of fear, worry, or grief to the surface so that you can release them. Rainbow Obsidian absorbs the heavy energy from your heart and offers you the comfort of knowing that you can get through the darkness and begin again.

ROSE QUARTZ surrounds you with the energy of unconditional love. It reminds you to love and support yourself every day during your pregnancy, no matter how you think you look or feel that day.

SELENITE clears and cleanses your space, creating a calm, positive atmosphere for your birth. You can also lay it over your chest at any time during your pregnancy to cleanse your energy of the day.

SMOKY QUARTZ allows you to let go of heavy emotions, limiting beliefs, and anxiety surrounding your fertility and pregnancy journey. It absorbs these feelings when they surface so that you can release them and move forward on your journey.

# FOR FERTILITY

MOONSTONE

PINK OPAL

CRYSTAL INTENTION

## I am healthy, happy, and fertile.

CRYSTAL PRACTICE

1   When you are ready to conceive, hold your crystals in your hands and say out loud, "I am healthy, happy, and fertile," 3 times.

2   Lie on your back and place your crystals accordingly:

MOONSTONE *below your belly button.*

PINK OPAL *over your heart.*

3   Leave your crystals on your body for 5 to 11 minutes. During this time, visualize how life will look and feel when you have a baby. Visualize yourself and your child—the sounds, the smells, and the feeling of holding your baby.

4   Place Pink Opal on your nightstand.

5   Keep Moonstone in your bra every day to keep its energy close by.

# DURING PREGNANCY

AMETHYST

ROSE QUARTZ

CRYSTAL INTENTION

## My baby and I are healthy.

CRYSTAL PRACTICE

1   Hold your crystals in your hands and say out loud, "My baby and I are healthy."

2   Every night before you go to bed, place Rose Quartz over your heart for love and Amethyst on your forehead to calm your mind, and then rub your belly.

3   Carry both crystals with you in your bra or pocket throughout your pregnancy.

## DURING BIRTH

AMETHYST

BLACK TOURMALINE

SELENITE

### CRYSTAL INTENTION

My body and my baby
know exactly what to do.

### CRYSTAL PRACTICE

1  One month before your
projected due date, hold your
crystals in your hands and say
out loud, "My body and my
baby know exactly what to do."
Keep them in a place where
they will be ready for
your delivery.

2  Bring your crystals with you
to the birth. Place them
accordingly in your room:

SELENITE *next to your
birthing area.*

AMETHYST *under your
birthing area.*

BLACK TOURMALINE *by your
birthing area, within reach. Take
one in each hand whenever you
want to feel protected.*

## HEALING FROM POSTPARTUM DEPRESSION

BLACK TOURMALINE

PINK OPAL

ROSE QUARTZ

### CRYSTAL INTENTION

I love my baby.

### CRYSTAL PRACTICE

1  Hold your crystals in your
hands and say out loud, "I love
my baby," 6 times.

2  Place Black Tourmaline and
Selenite next to your bathtub
and fill the tub with warm
water.

3  Place your Rose Quartz and
Pink Opal in your bath.

4  Add 1 cup sea salt and
anything else you want to
create a relaxing bath.

5  Once you're in the tub, place
Rose Quartz and Pink Opal
over your heart and close your
eyes. Breathe in love. Breathe
out fear. Breathe in trust.
Breathe out worry. Breathe in
happiness.

6  Relax in your bath for 10 to 20
minutes.

7  Repeat steps 1–6 once a week
for 3 to 6 months.

If your feelings of depression last for
more than a few days, or become
severe, we recommend seeking
medical assistance.

# GRIEVING AFTER A MISCARRIAGE

CARNELIAN

RAINBOW OBSIDIAN

SMOKY QUARTZ

## CRYSTAL INTENTION

**I can heal after loss.
It is not my fault.
I can become
pregnant again.**

## CRYSTAL PRACTICE

1 Hold your crystals in your hands and say out loud, "I can heal after loss. It is not my fault. I can become pregnant again," 9 times.

2 Lie on your back and place your crystals accordingly:

SMOKY QUARTZ *over your pubic bone.*

CARNELIAN *under your belly button.*

RAINBOW OBSIDIAN *over your heart.*

3 Leave your crystals on your body for 11 minutes. During this time, allow yourself to feel all your emotions of sadness, anger, and grief. Cry. Scream. Bring them all to the surface. Visualize your crystals absorbing them all so you don't have to hold on to them anymore.

4 When you're finished, place your crystals outside for 4 hours to cleanse.

5 Repeat steps 1–4 throughout your grieving process.

# getting focused

If you find yourself constantly distracted, it's time to get focused. When you tap into this state, you stay on course and productive, no matter what is going on around you. Focus also helps you overcome internal distractions, such as overactive thinking and daydreaming, so you can accomplish the task at hand. Use these crystals whenever you need to clear your mind and get laser focused.

AZURITE helps you expand your mind so you can increase your concentration. This stone inspires you to find creative ways to stay on target. It shifts your perspective and your mental state so you can move forward undisturbed and complete the task in front of you.

CLEAR QUARTZ enhances your mental clarity. Getting clear on your priorities and goals is the first step to acquiring better focus. When you know what it is you want to focus on, you're halfway there!

HEMATITE encourages you to get out of your head and into your body. Hematite helps you to feel rooted, stay centered, and maintain a strong mind-body connection so that you are not distracted by your surroundings. This stone's grounding nature is what you need to avoid mental overload and overstimulation.

CRYSTAL INTENTION

# I am focused.

CRYSTAL PRACTICE

1   Hold your crystals in your hands and say out loud, "I am focused." Repeat 3 times.

2   Lie on your back and place your crystals accordingly:

CLEAR QUARTZ *above the top of your head.*

AZURITE *in the middle of your forehead, slightly above your eyebrows.*

HEMATITE *in each hand.*

3   Lie with your crystals for 11 minutes. During this time, visualize your mind filling with bright, white light to calm any chaos in your mind. Feel the weight of the Hematite in your hands pulling any ungrounded energy in your body back down to the Earth.

# grounding
# yourself

When you are grounded, you are physically, emotionally, and spiritually centered, balanced, and secure. You feel as though you are in control of your life. You feel rooted and stable, as if you are a strong tree standing firmly and unwaveringly. When life events have you feeling frantic and unstable, it's time to connect with these crystals to strengthen your foundation.

HEMATITE connects you with the Earth's energy to feel as though your feet are planted firmly on the ground. This stone offers you a deep-rooted bond with nature, the most grounding force that exists. Due to its iron-based makeup, the weight of this crystal will keep you from feeling as if you are scattered, all over the place, or floating up into the clouds.

SHUNGITE detoxes you of anything that's preventing you from connecting with your foundation. When you maintain a strong founda-tion, it is harder to be knocked off your center. Shungite's energy neutralizes heavy emotions and energies that can leave you feeling ungrounded.

SMOKY QUARTZ helps you let go of negativity and unwanted energy so you can feel centered and balanced. Let this crystal absorb anything that does not serve you so you can focus on staying stable, secure, and grounded.

CRYSTAL INTENTION

## I am grounded.

CRYSTAL PRACTICE

1  Hold your crystals in both hands and say out loud, "I am grounded," 3 times.

2  Standing tall with both feet planted on the ground, place your crystals accordingly:

SMOKY QUARTZ *and* SHUNGITE *between your feet.*
HEMATITE *in each hand.*

3  Close your eyes and take 3 deep breaths.

4  Feel the weight of the crystals rooting you into the Earth and removing anything from your mind, body, or spirit that's preventing you from feeling grounded.

5  Set a timer for 3 to 5 minutes and breathe deeply while holding your crystals.

# increasing confidence

Feeling confident is being secure in who you are. You stand proudly in your body, recognize your abilities, and appreciate the characteristics that make you *you*. When you are confident, your truest, highest self shines through. Use this crystal combination when you want to bring confidence into everything you do.

CARNELIAN encourages you to act with certainty. It gives you the bold confidence to live life in an original, creative, and imaginative way.

CITRINE allows you to lighten up on self-criticism. This yellow crystal draws out your inner sunshine to replace any insecurity with contentment and confidence.

GARNET fills you with passion. When you love and feel excited about what you are doing, you exude confidence.

LAPIS LAZULI empowers you to lead with confidence. Whether you're paving the way for yourself or others, this stone allows you to do so with conviction and self-assurance.

RHODOCHROSITE encourages you to be confident in your worth. Self-love and self-confidence are directly related, and this crystal teaches you to value yourself and be confident in what you have to offer the world.

# I am confident.

1   Hold your crystals in your hands and say out loud, "I am confident," 3 times.

2   Lie on your back and place your crystals accordingly:

GARNET *over your pelvic bone.*

CARNELIAN *below your belly button.*

CITRINE *1 inch above your belly button.*

RHODOCHROSITE *over your heart.*

LAPIS LAZULI *on your forehead.*

3   Close your eyes and clear your mind.

4   Touch your Garnet with your dominant hand and say out loud, "I am confident."

5   Repeat step 4 with your Carnelian, then your Citrine, then your Rhodochrosite, and finally your Lapis Lazuli.

6   Lie with the crystals on your body for 11 minutes.

7   When you're done, place your Garnet, Citrine, Rhodochrosite, and Lapis Lazuli on a windowsill.

8   Carry your Carnelian in your bra or pocket during the day as a reminder of your intention.

# love

There are many types of love and each adds value to your life in a different way. Love brings happiness, joy, intimacy, and feelings of connectedness. But first you have to be open to it. Use these crystals to infuse love into all areas of your life.

AVENTURINE prepares you to be lucky in love by opening your heart. This stone works with the energy of the heart, clearing out the murky emotions you have stored and leaving space for brighter and newer love. That way, when your lucky energy brings a new relationship your way, you are ready for it.

BLACK KYANITE helps you cut away a toxic person. If you are in a relationship that drains you and doesn't serve you, this crystal helps you detach yourself from that person and that relationship.

CHRYSOPRASE encourages you to put down your phone and connect with your loved ones. It reminds you to be more present in your relationships and prioritize spending quality time with those around you.

GOLDEN HEALER QUARTZ allows you to stay in control of your emotions when heated conversations arise in your relationship. When you and your partner get into arguments, this stone helps you remain calm and collected so you can resolve the issue with less drama.

MALACHITE transforms your love life. A crystal of the heart, Malachite supports your quest to find true love by helping you identify old patterns that don't serve you.

OCEAN JASPER nurtures your spirit and reminds you that the number one person you must love is yourself. This stone helps you show yourself love by prioritizing your own wants and needs.

RAINBOW OBSIDIAN helps you grieve the loss of love. Allowing yourself to feel the pain from a breakup or separation is a necessary part of the healing process. Use this crystal to help you bring up any negative emotions so you can release them and move forward.

RHODONITE reminds you to embrace a forgiving nature. If your partner says or does something hurtful, let this crystal be your reminder to approach the situation with calm, love, and understanding.

ROSE QUARTZ carries the gentle energy of unconditional love. Its soft pink color leaves you with a physical reminder to be tender and kind to others and yourself. This stone brings the energy of love to everything it comes into contact with.

SUNSTONE heats things up in the bedroom. Its spicy energy reduces your inhibitions and enhances your sex life. Sunstone gives you the confidence to speak up, try new things, and be spontaneous.

# STAYING CONNECTED IN COMMITTED RELATIONSHIPS

CHRYSOPRASE
GOLDEN HEALER QUARTZ
RHODONITE
SUNSTONE

### CRYSTAL INTENTION

## I love you unconditionally.

### CRYSTAL PRACTICE

1 In your bedroom, hold Rhodonite and Sunstone in your hands, and have your partner hold Chrysoprase and Golden Healer in their hands. Say out loud together, "I love you unconditionally," 6 times.

2 Place your Sunstone on your nightstand.

3 Sit face-to-face and place the Golden Healer Quartz in between you.

4 Take turns sharing out loud 3 things that you each love and appreciate about the other.

5 Give each other a long-lasting hug.

6 When you're finished, place your crystals on your dresser.

# ATTRACTING LOVE (DATING)

AVENTURINE
MALACHITE
ROSE QUARTZ

### CRYSTAL INTENTION

## I attract love.

### CRYSTAL PRACTICE

1 Hold your crystals in both hands and say out loud, "I attract love," 6 times.

2 Place a piece of Malachite and a piece of Rose Quartz together on your bedroom nightstand to represent 2 people in a loving relationship.

3 Before going to bed, place your Rose Quartz over your heart for 11 minutes to open and infuse it with love.

4 When you go on a date, carry Aventurine and Rose Quartz together in your bra or pocket.

# HEALING FROM BREAKUPS AND SEPARATION

BLACK KYANITE

RAINBOW OBSIDIAN

## CRYSTAL INTENTION

**I release all the heaviness within my heart. I will heal from this.**

## CRYSTAL PRACTICE

1   Hold your crystals in both hands and say out loud, "I release all the heaviness within my heart. I will heal from this," 9 times.

2   Holding your Black Kyanite in your non-writing hand, write down the good, the bad, and the ugly. Write down your fear, anger, sorrow, frustration—any emotions that come up—just get them out and onto the paper.

3   When you're finished, rip up your paper and throw it away.

4   With your Black Kyanite in your dominant hand, move your crystal in a slicing motion approximately 5 inches in front of your heart and cut away the hurtful emotions, person, and/ or relationship. Do this 3 times.

5   Lie on your back and place your Rainbow Obsidian over your heart. Close your eyes and leave your crystal on your body for 11 minutes. Allow yourself space to process your emotions and grieve.

6   When you're finished, place your crystals in the Sun for 4 hours to cleanse.

7   Repeat steps 1–6 while you heal from your breakup.

# FOSTERING SELF-LOVE

OCEAN JASPER

ROSE QUARTZ

## CRYSTAL INTENTION

**I love myself unconditionally.**

## CRYSTAL PRACTICE

1   Hold your crystals in both hands and say out loud, "I love myself unconditionally," 6 times.

2   Standing in front of a mirror, hold Ocean Jasper and Rose Quartz over your heart and state 1 thing you love about yourself. Then state 1 thing you are going to do today to prioritize yourself.

3   Carry these stones with you in your bra or pocket throughout the day and place them together next to your bed at night.

4   Repeat steps 1–3 daily.

# managing
# your anger

Learning to manage anger is a critical part of developing healthy relationships with family, friends, and co-workers. Unresolved anger can disrupt your life, but when you are able to control it, you can maintain a healthy mind, body, and spirit. Use these crystals when you want to release your anger responsibly.

———

ARAGONITE helps to break through resentments and unresolved emotions. This stone encourages you to process your feelings and release your anger before your heated emotions take control.

BLACK TOURMALINE absorbs the chaotic and negative energy around you so you do not dwell in anger.

HEMATITE grounds you in your power so that you can express yourself assertively instead of aggressively.

SELENITE purifies your mind, helping you arrive at a middle ground where you can see the situation clearly. Connecting with it allows you to return to a calmer state of mind.

# I release my anger.

1   Hold the crystals in your hands and state out loud, "I release my anger," 3 times.

2   Standing with both your feet firmly planted on the ground, place your Black Tourmaline on the ground in between your feet. Hold 1 piece of Aragonite and 1 piece of Hematite in your right hand, and 1 piece of Aragonite and 1 piece of Hematite in your left hand.

3   Close your eyes and take 5 deep breaths.

4   Picture the person or situation that is causing your anger standing in front of you. Say whatever it is that you want to say to them or about the situation. Don't hold back.

5   Breathe deeply for 3 to 5 minutes. Squeeze your crystals and visualize your anger, negativity, and explosive energy being absorbed into the crystals and into the Earth. As you breathe in and out, feel your anger dissipate.

6   When you're finished, place your Aragonite and Hematite on the ground next to your Black Tourmaline.

7   Pick up your Selenite and place it over your chest. Visualize bright, white light filling up the space where your anger resided. Hold your Selenite over your chest for 3 to 5 minutes and breathe. Feel yourself becoming calmer with each breath.

8   After you're done, cleanse your crystals to remove any energy that they have absorbed so they are ready to use again.

# mastering communication

Being a good communicator is the key to success in both your personal and professional life. Whether you're giving a presentation at work, speaking to a group, or trying to get a point across to your children, being able to express yourself clearly and confidently is essential for communication. Use these crystals when you want to communicate clearly in every aspect of your life.

AQUAMARINE aids in verbal expression and dissolves unnecessary stress from your mind. It is particularly useful for public speaking, encouraging you to express yourself with honesty and authenticity.

CARNELIAN is excellent for overcoming stage fright or fear of the unexpected. It helps you to be more confident in the spotlight with people listening to what you have to say.

LAPIS LAZULI reminds you that words are powerful, and it is important to think before you speak. Conscious communication allows you to speak thoughtfully so you don't say something you wish you hadn't.

MALACHITE helps you to get out of your head and speak from your heart. It transforms your words so you are able to articulate your meaning more clearly and ensure that your words match your intent.

SODALITE encourages you to keep your words fluid and concise. It clears your mind, helping you stay focused so that you don't become distracted or lose your train of thought.

# I communicate clearly.

## CRYSTAL PRACTICE

1   Hold your crystals in your hands and say out loud, "I communicate clearly," 3 times.

2   Lie on your back and place your crystals accordingly:

MALACHITE *over your heart.*

SODALITE *over your throat.*

AQUAMARINE *between your eyebrows.*

3   Leave your crystals on your body for 11 minutes. During this time, visualize yourself speaking clearly and see others responding positively to what you have to say.

IF YOU HAVE A PUBLIC SPEAKING ENGAGEMENT: *Carry Carnelian with you in your bra or pocket or wear it as a necklace for extra courage and confidence.*

IF YOU KNOW THE CONVERSATION MAY GET HEATED: *Carry Lapis Lazuli as a touchstone to remind you to think before you speak to lead you to the best outcome.*

# overcoming fear

Fear is a necessary feeling that prevents you from getting into a dangerous situation. However, chronic and toxic fear can restrict your life to the point that you aren't living to your full potential. Learning to overcome fear begins with changing your attitude. When you realize that you have the power to release your fear, it will no longer restrict you, and you can start living the way you are meant to. Use these crystals when you are ready to conquer your fears.

LEPIDOLITE calms any anxiety brought up by fear. This stone brings peace to your mind and soothes your worries so that you aren't gripped by fear.

SMOKY QUARTZ helps you let go of negative feelings that arise from fear. By allowing these emotions to pass through you without taking hold of you, you gain back control of your life.

TIGER'S EYE gives you the courage to overcome your fear. For those times when you just can't help but be afraid, Tiger's Eye helps you to conquer your fear.

TOURMALINATED QUARTZ brings awareness to the dark emotions that arise when you are controlled by fear so you can turn your fear into strength. Once you are able to see the situation differently, fear becomes easier to manage.

CRYSTAL INTENTION

## I release my fear.

CRYSTAL PRACTICE

1   Ask yourself, *What am I afraid of?* Once you have your fear in mind, hold the crystals in both hands and state out loud, "I release my fears." Repeat 3 times.

2   Lie on your back and place your crystals accordingly:

SMOKY QUARTZ *over the pubic bone.*

TIGER'S EYE *over your belly button.*

TOURMALINATED QUARTZ *on the center of your chest*

LEPIDOLITE *in the center of your forehead, slightly above your eyebrows.*

3   Take 5 deep breaths and visualize your fears being absorbed into the energy of the Earth.

4   Lie with these crystals on your body for 3 to 5 minutes. Throughout this time, affirm to yourself that you are fearless.

# pets

Pets can benefit from the energy of crystals just like people!
Whether your pet has anxiety, behavioral problems, or more
physical issues, crystals can help enhance your pet's well-
being and longevity. Use these crystals when your beloved
pet could benefit from healing energy.

AGATE restores balance and brings your pet's mind, body, and spirit back into equilibrium. When everything is brought back into alignment, pain and negative behaviors can be minimized.

AMETHYST encourages a state of peace and relaxation to relieve pain. Whether your pet has joint pain or arthritis, this crystal works to release any negative energy that may be contributing to your pet's discomfort.

BLACK TOURMALINE allows your pet to feel safe, secure, and taken care of. This newfound sense of security is especially helpful for rescue pets.

BLUE LACE AGATE helps to calm an overly anxious or stressed-out pet. This stone rebalances your pet's energy field and quiets rattled nerves. If your pet is acting up or shutting down, Blue Lace Agate will help your pet feel safe and secure.

HEMATITE keeps your pet feeling grounded and balanced. It helps to alleviate feelings of anxiety and nervousness, especially when you are away.

LEPIDOLITE soothes your pet's anxiety. It encourages a calm and relaxed state of mind.

ROSE QUARTZ is a soothing crystal for rescue animals. Its loving energy works to temper the effects of past abuse. This stone helps to dissolve any fear your pet may still harbor and replaces it with feelings of love. Rose Quartz also helps your pet begin to adapt to and love their forever home.

SELENITE cleanses and purifies your pet's energy when your pet is not feeling well physically and emotionally. Even pets need to be cleansed of negative energy, whether it's a recent bad encounter with another person or pet or the harmful memories that a rescue animal may carry with them. This crystal infuses your pet with light to restore their vibrant, bright, and happy energy.

## You are safe, loved, and taken care of.

# FOR EVERYDAY USE

ROSE QUARTZ

SELENITE

### CRYSTAL PRACTICE

1  Hold your crystals in your hands and say out loud, "You are safe, loved, and taken care of."

2  Place a piece of Rose Quartz next to your pet's water bowl, in their crate, or in their aquarium.

3  Place a large piece of Selenite next to your pet's bed.

4  Smile at your pet every day! And, of course, tell them you love them!

# FOR RESCUED PETS

BLACK TOURMALINE

ROSE QUARTZ

### CRYSTAL PRACTICE

1  Hold your crystals in your hands and say out loud, "You are safe, loved, and taken care of."

2  Place a piece of Rose Quartz and a piece of Black Tourmaline next to your pet's crate or bed so that your pet is close to them throughout the day.

## FOR RELIEVING PAIN

AGATE

AMETHYST

CRYSTAL PRACTICE

1 Hold your crystals in your hands and say out loud, "You are pain free."

2 Have your pet lie down in a comfortable position.

3 With one hand, place or hold these two crystals over the area of pain. With your other hand, continue to stroke and soothe them.

4 Continue this action until your pet is relaxed.

## FOR SOOTHING NERVOUSNESS OR ANXIETY

BLUE LACE AGATE

LEPIDOLITE

CRYSTAL PRACTICE

1 Hold your crystals in your hands and say out loud, "You are safe, calm, and relaxed."

2 Have your pet lie down in a comfortable position.

3 Place the Lepidolite near their head.

4 Gently rub the Blue Lace Agate on your pet's belly, forehead, and neck repeatedly.

5 Repeat until they are in a calmer state of mind.

## FOR SEPARATION ANXIETY

HEMATITE

SELENITE

CRYSTAL PRACTICE

1 Hold your crystals in your hands and say out loud, "You are safe, calm, and relaxed."

2 Before you leave, have your pet lie down in a comfortable position.

3 Holding your Selenite in your dominant hand, gently "comb" the crystal around your pet's body to clear any nervousness or anxiety.

4 Place Hematite next to their water bowl or in their crate to help them feel secure and grounded.

# protection

Protection offers you a feeling of security and safety that allows you to move through the world without being affected by unwanted, low vibrational energy. Use these crystal combinations in your home, office, and car to promote a constant state of energetic protection.

AMETHYST helps to promote safety and to keep your car running smoothly.

BLACK KYANITE cuts the cords with other people's toxic energy. If you've ever felt bad energy coming from someone in a bad mood, this is the kind of toxic energy that tends to spread. Use Black Kyanite to energetically detach from anyone whose negative energy spreads to you.

BLACK TOURMALINE creates a protective energy shield around you and your space. Use this stone as a force field of protection to ward off theft and vandalism and to keep all the bad vibes from entering your personal space or environment. Black Tourmaline also helps to dispel negative energy, especially from arguments, bad moods, or road rage.

CLEAR QUARTZ acts as a force field of white light to surround your space, especially your car. It reminds you to be crystal clear and focused on the road while driving.

LAPIS LAZULI allows you to step into your power and tap into your inner wisdom. This stone leaves you feeling strong, secure, and protected as you go about your day.

SELENITE is a master stone for purifying unwanted energy. To prevent any kind of negative energetic buildup from the energy you accumulate all day long, use this crystal to constantly cleanse you and your space.

TOURMALINATED QUARTZ is known to remove negative and stuck energy, leaving space for lighter energy to take its place. Whether it's working against negative thoughts or feelings, Tourmalinated Quartz protects your energy and teaches you to transform anything that doesn't serve you into something more positive.

# PROTECTING YOUR HOME OR OFFICE

BLACK KYANITE

BLACK TOURMALINE

SELENITE

TOURMALINATED QUARTZ

## CRYSTAL INTENTION

### I am protected.

## CRYSTAL PRACTICE

1   Hold your crystals in both hands and say out loud, "I am protected," 3 times.

2   Place Black Tourmaline outside your home on either side of any entryway to protect your space.

3   Place Black Kyanite, Selenite, and Tourmalinated Quartz on the windowsill of any room in which you feel you need extra energetic protection.

4   Cleanse your crystals weekly to remove any energy they've absorbed and put them back in place.

# PROTECTING YOUR ENERGY ON THE GO

BLACK KYANITE

BLACK TOURMALINE

LAPIS LAZULI

## CRYSTAL INTENTION

### I am protected.

## CRYSTAL PRACTICE

1   Hold your crystals in both hands and say out loud, "I am protected," 3 times.

2   Holding your Black Kyanite in your dominant hand, use it to draw a circle around your body to set a strong boundary.

3   Carry Black Tourmaline and Lapis Lazuli in your bra or pocket throughout the day.

# PROTECTING YOU AND YOUR CAR WHILE DRIVING

**CRYSTAL INTENTION**

## I am protected inside my car.

**CRYSTAL PRACTICE**

1   Clean your car, inside and out. Remove all extra clothes and clutter.

2   Before you start your engine, hold your crystals in both hands and say out loud, "I am protected. My car is protected. Everyone in my car is protected at all times. Each and every day, a shield of white light surrounds my car to protect it and keep it safe."

3   Place your Black Tourmaline under the driver's seat for protection.

4   Place Selenite under the passenger's seat for cleansing.

5   Place Clear Quartz in the center console to create a shield of white light.

6   Place Amethyst in your glove compartment to keep your car running smoothly.

7   Every 3 months, gather your crystals, cleanse them, and place them back inside the car.

# reducing EMF sensitivity

Electromagnetic fields (EMFs) come from electronic devices like computers, laptops, mobile phones, tablets, and microwaves, as well as wireless networks (Wi-Fi) and Bluetooth devices. Radio frequency (RF) radiation is also emitted from Wi-Fi and Bluetooth. If you have a sensitivity to EMFs and RFs, you may experience physical symptoms such as joint and muscle pain, fatigue, and insomnia when exposed to them for extended periods of time. Use these crystals to create protection from the harmful effects of EMFs and RFs.

BLACK TOURMALINE absorbs negative energy from EMFs and RFs. It enhances the human body's own protective electrical field, thereby creating a stronger deterrent against harmful EMF and RF radiation.

SELENITE cleanses your body, your environment, and the layer of electromagnetic "dirt" that builds up in your energy field. By purifying the area in which you live and work, this crystal prevents the harmful effects from compounding around and within you.

SHUNGITE works to neutralize the "smog" that comes from electromagnetic devices. This stone detoxifies you of the harmful radiations so they don't linger or build up in your physical body. When possible, always use Elite Shungite, as it will have a stronger effect when it comes to EMFs.

# I am protected from the effects of EMFs and RFs.

CRYSTAL PRACTICE

1    Hold all crystals in your hands and state out loud, "I am protected from the effects of EMFs and RFs," 3 times.

2    Place a Shungite in the four corners of any room that has an abundance of EMFs in it. This will help to neutralize their effects.

3    Place Black Tourmaline and Shungite at the base of computers, microwaves, or around any of your home electronic devices. This will work to block out some of the EMF output.

4    Place your Selenite under your desk (at home and work). Place your bare feet on top of it to fill your body with purifying and cleansing energy.

5    Repeat steps 1–4 daily.

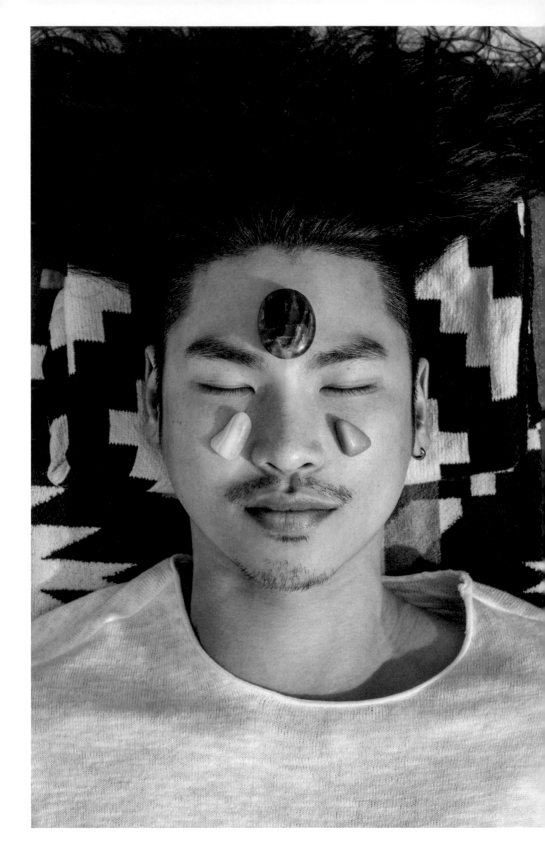

# releasing stress

Stress can affect your emotional, spiritual, and physical bodies, wearing each of them down to the point of exhaustion and poor health. Although a stress-free life is ideal, it's not always realistic. You juggle your job, your relationships, and your personal endeavors all day long, some of which are bound to cause you stress. But learning to manage your stress levels will help to resolve its effects so they don't build up and prevent you from living your best life.

AMETHYST brings deep peace and relaxation to your mind, body, and spirit to help diminish feelings of stress.

ANGELITE quells stress with its reassuring and comforting energy. Thought to connect you with the angelic realm, this stone reminds you that support is always available to you.

BLUE LACE AGATE helps to manage and reduce stress levels. With just one look, the blue hues of this stone begin to calm you down. This crystal encourages you to take a deep breath and return to a state of tranquility.

FLUORITE dispels chaotic thoughts and excess mind chatter. It has a stable, peaceful, and positive energy that combats stressful thoughts.

LEPIDOLITE brings awareness to your stressors so you can address them and prevent yourself from spinning out of control. It helps to calm your nerves and ease your worried mind.

# I am stress free.
# I am now calm and relaxed.

1 Hold your crystals in both hands and state out loud, "I am stress free. I am now calm and relaxed," 9 times.

2 Lie on your back and place your crystals accordingly:

BLUE LACE AGATE *on your right cheek and* ANGELITE *on your left cheek.*

FLUORITE *over your forehead in between your eyebrows.*

AMETHYST *in your right hand and* LEPIDOLITE *in your left hand.*

3 Set a timer for 5 to 11 minutes and breathe deeply. During this time, visualize the crystals absorbing any stress, anxiety, or tension that has accumulated throughout your day.

# relieving
# pain

Pain can interrupt daily life and responsibilities, as well as wreak havoc on your mental and emotional state. Whether it's acute or chronic pain, being able to find some relief for your physical body can work wonders for your energetic body. Get your life back by relieving yourself of pain.

AMETHYST is one of the best crystals for relieving pain, especially from headaches and arthritis. This stone works on a subtle level to release any negative energy that may be contributing to your pain. Connect with it to encourage a state of peace and relaxation as your pain subsides.

SELENITE cleanses and purifies the body of stuck or stagnant energy that causes energetic blocks, which can translate to physical discomfort. It is believed to emit a healing white light that regenerates cells and works to clear the pain and restore your body to its initial state.

SHUNGITE is thought to reverse the effects of "free radicals" and to heal and repair your body on a cellular level. It helps to detoxify your mind, body, and spirit of anything that is contributing to your pain, bringing everything back into alignment.

CRYSTAL INTENTION

## I am pain free.

CRYSTAL PRACTICE

1   Hold your crystals in both hands and state out loud, "I am pain free," 7 times.

2   Sit or lie down in the position that is most comfortable to you, and place your crystals accordingly:

SELENITE *over your chest or over your back.*

AMETHYST *and* SHUNGITE *directly on your area of pain.*

3   Leave your crystals on your body for 11 minutes. During this time, visualize the pain leaving your body.

4   After you're done, place your crystals outside in the light for 4 hours to cleanse.

5   For ongoing pain, repeat steps 1–4 as needed.

# removing obstacles

Many external obstacles are out of your control, and you cannot always control the actions of others. However, there are certain obstacles to success that you do have control over, such as your mind-set, behavioral patterns, habits, and how you spend your time and energy. When you are getting in your own way of being successful, it is time to remove any obstacles that you are creating for yourself. Connect with this crystal combination to clear your way and move forward with grace and ease.

CITRINE reminds you to stay in the light. This stone does not hold on to dark energy and encourages you to release the dense, heavy energy that darkens your mood so you can stay bright, cheery, and happy.

PHANTOM QUARTZ inspires you to break through limiting mind-sets that are holding you back from reaching your goals. It encourages you to find a new way to move forward when you encounter resistance.

SMOKY QUARTZ allows you to let go and release what no longer serves you. Carrying around old energetic baggage creates a buildup of negative emotions that continue to affect your life. This stone helps you move forward.

TIGER'S EYE helps you shift your perspective when you feel stuck. When you feel frustration building, it will remind you to open your eyes to the possibilties that are always around you.

# My path is clear.

1   Write down on a piece of paper the internal or habitual obstacle you are ready to move past (e.g., limiting belief, negative thought pattern, pessimistic mind-set, etc.).

2   Hold your crystals in your hands and say out loud,

"I remove _____."
*(State the obstacle you have chosen.)*
Repeat 8 more times.

3   Write down what your life will look like and how your life will change once you move past the obstacle.

4   Then write down one action you can take today to begin breaking through that obstacle.

5   Place the Citrine, Phantom Quartz, and Tiger's Eye on top of the paper.

6   Carry Smoky Quartz with you daily in your pocket until you break through your obstacle.

# sleep

Restful sleep is a key component of your health and well-being on every level—physical, mental, emotional, and spiritual. Maintaining healthy and regular sleep patterns should be one of your top priorities. Use these crystals to support mindful sleep habits.

AGATE creates balance in your mind, body, spirit, and space. When you feel more balanced, you are able to get a better night's rest.

AMETHYST pacifies an overactive mind. It emits a strong tranquil vibration that will soothe your turbulent mentality.

CELESTITE fills your room with a harmonious energy. This stone is especially good for children and babies because of its pacifying effects, which help lull them to sleep. Adults will also gain the same effects from this subtle blue crystal.

LABRADORITE helps you to fall into a deep sleep and tap into the limitless potential of your dream state. For sleep to be truly rejuvenating, you need to sleep soundly, without interruption.

SELENITE cleanses your mind, body, and spirit, as well as your bedroom. Its gentle, pure energy will work wonders for a restful night's sleep.

# RESTFUL SLEEP

AGATE

AMETHYST

CELESTITE

LABRADORITE

SELENITE

### CRYSTAL INTENTION

## I sleep soundly.

### CRYSTAL PRACTICE

1   Hold your crystals in your hands and say out loud, "I sleep soundly," 9 times.

2   Place your crystals accordingly in your bedroom:

AMETHYST *and* LABRADORITE *on your nightstand.*

SELENITE *underneath your bed.*

AGATE *underneath your pillow.*

CELESTITE *on the windowsill.*

3   Cleanse your crystals once a week to remove any energy they've absorbed and to be ready to use again.

# SOOTHING INSOMNIA

Before you begin using your crystals to soothe your insomnia, it's important to take a deeper look at the energy in your bedroom and go through this bedroom checklist. After you've addressed the items on the checklist, you can bring in Selenite and Celestite.

## Bedroom Checklist

**DO YOU HAVE A MIRROR, COMPUTER, OR TV IN YOUR BEDROOM?** Ideally, keep mirrors, TVs, and computers out of your bedroom. Reflective surfaces like mirrors double the energy in your room. This same energy bounces back and forth throughout the night, staying active while you sleep. If you cannot remove them completely, try covering all of the mirrors and electronic devices with a sheet or curtain.

**IS YOUR ROOM CLUTTERED?** Bedrooms filled with clutter make your mind feel cluttered, which makes it hard to sleep.

**HAVE YOU CLEANSED YOUR BEDROOM LATELY?** Not cleaned, but energetically cleansed? If the answer is no, give it a thorough cleansing with sound or by burning sage.

## CRYSTAL INTENTION

# I fall asleep easily.

### CRYSTAL PRACTICE

1  Go through the bedroom checklist just described.

2  Hold your Selenite and Celestite in both hands and state out loud, "I fall asleep easily."

3  Place your Celestite on your nightstand.

4  Place multiple pieces of Selenite around the perimeter of your bed to cleanse and calm the energy of your space.

5  Before you go to bed, lay a piece of Selenite over your chest for 5 to 11 minutes to clear away the endless mind chatter.

6  When you are finished, place your Selenite on your nightstand. Close your eyes, breathe deeply, and begin to drift off to sleep.

7  Cleanse your crystals once a week to remove any energy they've absorbed and then repeat steps 1–6 until your insomnia passes.

# strengthening willpower

Willpower is having the control to do or not do something, even when it's difficult. When you have willpower, you have the ability to stay on track with what you've decided you want even when it's easier to break your commitment. Whether it's internal or external forces that threaten to get you off track, a strong will works to keep you motivated and dedicated. Use these crystals to strengthen your willpower.

BLACK KYANITE helps you cut away any self-sabotaging thoughts. Say good-bye to the voice in your head that's telling you that *you* can't, because *you* can. You have the will to make the changes you want to see.

CITRINE brings light to challenging situations, reminding you to stay positive on your journey. Use it as you give yourself affirmations and remember to enjoy life, even as you purposefully pursue your goals.

GARNET inspires you to be passionate about the track you're on. When you are excited, revved up, and passionate about your decisions and choices, it's much easier to stick with them.

TIGER'S EYE gives you the courage to venture into the uncomfortable. Making changes to your routine can be difficult, but this stone gives you the bravery to push through the challenge.

# My willpower is strong.

1   Identify what you want to have more willpower with (e.g., a goal, overcoming an addiction, establishing a new habit, etc.).

2   Bring to mind any thoughts, beliefs, or actions that are holding you back from what you want to achieve.

3   With your Black Kyanite in your dominant hand, move your crystal in a slicing motion approximately 5 inches in front of your forehead and cut the thought away 3 times.

4   Hold your Citrine, Garnet, and Tiger's Eye in your hands and say out loud, "My willpower is strong. For the next 21 days,

I will _____."
*(Fill in the blank with what you want to achieve.)*
Repeat 2 more times.

5   Carry Citrine, Garnet, and Tiger's Eye in your pocket as a reminder to have the will to stay committed. If you feel your willpower weaken, squeeze your crystals.

# tackling weight loss

Losing weight can be an emotional roller-coaster ride.
Oftentimes, weight gain shows up due to emotional
baggage. Addressing long-held emotions and beliefs will not
only make you healthier and happier, but it can also support
your endeavor to reach your ideal weight. Use these crystals
to support your weight-loss journey.

APATITE is aptly named for its ability to help you suppress your appetite. This crystal inspires you to stay on track with your weight-loss goals. If you have trouble sticking to a diet or eating to nourish your body, this stone will help you stay strong.

CITRINE keeps your spirits high during your weight-loss journey. Rather than getting down on yourself and beating yourself up, this happy stone reminds you to be content with yourself no matter where you are in your journey.

CLEAR QUARTZ helps you get clear on your weight-loss goals. *Is there a specific amount of weight you want to lose? Do you want to eat a specific way or work out a certain number of times per week?* Use it to gain clarity on what goals you need to set to achieve your ideal weight loss.

SHUNGITE supports the physical act of losing weight. This stone contains antioxidants, which help to boost energy levels, increase metabolism, and decrease inflammation in the body. Note: when using Shungite specifically in your drinking water, always use Elite Shungite.

TURQUOISE promotes overall health and works to ensure that you lose weight in a healthy and sustainable way. It reminds you that your health and well-being is more important than looking a certain way or seeing a specific number on the scale.

# I am losing weight.

1   Hold the crystals in both hands and state out loud, "I am losing weight."

2   Write down your weight-loss goals on a piece of paper and place Clear Quartz on top of the paper.

3   Place Elite Shungite in a glass of water and let it sit for at least 4 hours. First thing in the morning, drink the Elite Shungite water. When you're finished, refill for the next day.

4   Place Citrine in your kitchen, dining room, or wherever you eat as a reminder to be happy.

5   Carry Apatite and Turquoise in your pocket every day to stay on track.

6   Repeat steps 1–5 until your goal is met.

# taking control of your health

Being healthy means taking care of yourself and feeling good in your mind and body. Health applies to not only the physical body, but the emotional and spiritual bodies as well. Maintaining your health or healing from a health challenge is a daily commitment, one that takes physical and mental determination. Use these crystals to support your health journey.

BLOODSTONE gets the energy moving throughout your body. It emits a strong vibration that is connected to your heart to help to promote circulation of energy throughout the body.

CLEAR QUARTZ gives you clarity on your health goals. When you are able to visualize your goals, your mind and body can begin to work toward them.

HEMATITE grounds your energy so you can focus on your health.

MALACHITE helps you to transform your health. This stone brings awareness to the choices you make and patterns you have that do not serve your overall health and well-being. Malachite encourages you make different choices that better serve you.

TURQUOISE reminds you to prioritize your health. It's easy to ignore your well-being temporarily. But eventually, if you ignore your health for too long, your body will force you to listen. Turquoise can get you back on track before you lose control of your health.

# I am healthy.

1   Hold all the crystals in your hands and state your intention out loud, "I am healthy," 7 times.

2   Lie on your back and place your crystals accordingly:

HEMATITE *over your pubic bone.*

BLOODSTONE *under your belly button.*

MALACHITE *over your heart.*

TURQUOISE *over your throat.*

CLEAR QUARTZ *on your forehead in between your eyebrows.*

3   Set a timer for 5 to 11 minutes and breathe deeply. During this time, visualize every cell of your being in radiant health.

# tapping into creativity

Not just for artists, creativity is simply using your imagination to develop something original. Whenever you're feeling uninspired, unenthused, or stuck, connecting to your creative side will give you the push you need to produce your best work.

———

ANGEL AURA QUARTZ encourages you to find the fun in your creative process. By bringing a playful attitude back into your project, you will shift your perspective and see things in an entirely new light.

CARNELIAN awakens hidden talents. The deep red and orange hues of this stone will bring the creative powers that exist within you to the surface.

RED JASPER encourages you to follow through with your creation. When you feel unmotivated, it is difficult to produce anything. This crystal will spur you into action so you can create what you set out to do.

TIGER'S EYE helps you find the courage to move past limitations and fears. Once you decide to embrace your creative prowess, it will help you bring it into the world with confidence.

# I am creative.

1  Flip through magazines or search the Internet to find 5 inspiring images that get your creative juices flowing. Cut or print them out.

2  Glue or tape the images to a piece of paper to create a mini creativity vision board.

3  Hold your crystals in both hands and say out loud, "I am creative."

4  Find space where your vision board can live; ideally it is in a space where you create.

5  Place your crystals accordingly on top of your vision board to charge it:

CARNELIAN *on the top.*

ANGEL AURA QUARTZ *on the bottom.*

TIGER'S EYE *on the left side.*

RED JASPER *on the right side.*

6  Look at your creativity vision board daily to be inspired to start a new creative project.

# travel

Traveling is always an adventure. It's exhilarating, it's fun, and it opens your mind to new experiences. But it can also be tiring and frustrating. From lines at the airport to difficulty navigating a new place, so much of the journey is physically and emotionally taxing. Use these crystals to stay energized, calm, and flexible and make the most out of your trip.

AGATE helps you to stay balanced while you travel. When you are in a new place and away from your regular routine, it is easy to feel out of sorts and off balance. Connecting with Agate gets you realigned and feeling centered.

AMETHYST encourages you to sit back, relax, and enjoy the vacation. It urges you to revel in your adventure and not get caught up in worry or tension.

ANGELITE soothes and supports you while traveling. It reminds you that you are not alone and your vehicle is surrounded with protective energy during your journey.

AQUAMARINE calms any fears related to flying or traveling over water. This stone helps you to accept and conquer your fears by providing peace and protection during travel, especially overseas.

BLACK TOURMALINE offers energetic protection on your excursions. It creates a barrier around you to shield you from bad vibes coming from anyone you encounter along the way.

CHRYSOPRASE reminds you to stay connected and present during your journey. It is easy to want to capture every moment of it with photos and video, but then you miss out on being 100 percent present in the experience. Chrysoprase encourages you to engage fully in every second of your trip.

LEMURIAN QUARTZ reminds you to have patience while you travel. When flights get delayed, tensions arise, and encounters go wrong, this crystal reminds you to remain calm and patient. It gives aid when things don't go exactly as planned.

MALACHITE helps to transform your state of mind to alleviate the effects of jet lag.

MOONSTONE has long held a reputation as a traveler's stone because it protects you (and your luggage) throughout your travel until you reach your destination.

SHUNGITE emits a protective energy that is especially effective when going through security at airports. This crystal helps to limit your exposure to harmful EMFs from scanning systems and electronic devices.

UNAKITE reminds you to be grateful for every experience while traveling. Through all the ups and any downs, enjoy each moment and know that everything will happen in divine timing.

# FOR PROTECTION WHILE TRAVELING

BLACK TOURMALINE

MOONSTONE

### CRYSTAL INTENTION

## I am safe and protected while traveling.

### CRYSTAL PRACTICE

1 Before you head to the airport, hold your crystals in both hands and say out loud, "I am safe and protected while traveling."

2 Place your Moonstone and Black Tourmaline in your luggage.

3 When you arrive at your destination and unpack your suitcase, keep your Moonstone in your luggage.

4 Carry your Black Tourmaline with you in your pocket wherever you go during your trip.

# FOR EMF PROTECTION AT THE AIRPORT

BLACK TOURMALINE

SHUNGITE

### CRYSTAL INTENTION

## I am shielded from EMFs.

### CRYSTAL PRACTICE

1 Before you head to the airport, hold your crystals in both hands and say out loud, "I am shielded from EMFs."

2 Place Shungite in one pocket and Black Tourmaline in the other. The crystals will absorb and neutralize EMFs before and after you walk through the scanner. (You can take these out as you go through security.)

3 Keep them in your pockets throughout the entire time you're at the airport.

# FOR PATIENCE
# WITH DELAYS

AMETHYST

LEMURIAN QUARTZ

### CRYSTAL INTENTION

## I practice patience.

### CRYSTAL PRACTICE

1  Before you begin traveling, hold your crystals in both hands and say out loud, "I practice patience."

2  Keep both your crystals in your pocket while traveling.

3  When faced with a delay, take your Lemurian Quartz out of your pocket and hold it in your dominant hand. Rub your thumb up and down the striations to keep yourself calm and relaxed.

# FOR FEAR
# OF FLYING

ANGELITE

AQUAMARINE

### CRYSTAL INTENTION

## I am calm, safe, and protected.

### CRYSTAL PRACTICE

1  Before takeoff, hold your crystals in both hands and say out loud, "I am calm, safe, and protected."

2  During the flight, hold and rub your stones to know that your angels surround you and the plane is protected.

3  During times of turbulence, give them a good, hard squeeze until the rough air passes.

# FOR JET LAG

AGATE

MALACHITE

## CRYSTAL INTENTION

### My internal clock adapts easily.

## CRYSTAL PRACTICE

1  When you get to your destination, hold your crystals in both hands and say out loud, "My internal clock adapts easily."

2  Drink a glass of water to get hydrated.

3  Holding one crystal in each hand, close your eyes and breathe deeply in and out. Use this time to reconnect with your breath and reconnect with your center.

4  Repeat steps 1–3 daily as needed as your body acclimates.

# TO STAY PRESENT AND CONNECTED WHILE TRAVELING

AMETHYST

CHRYSOPRASE

UNAKITE

## CRYSTAL INTENTION

### I am on a wonderful adventure.

## CRYSTAL PRACTICE

1  When you get to your destination, hold your crystals in both hands and say out loud, "I am on a wonderful adventure."

2  Take a moment to close your eyes. Connect with your breath and have a moment of gratitude for the adventure that is awaiting you. Connect with the place you are in and be present in the experience.

3  Open your eyes, and place your crystals on your nightstand as a visual reminder of your intention.

4  Carry your Chrysoprase in your pocket with you daily, wherever you go.

# wealth

Creating wealth is a three-step process. First, you have to build a healthy money mind-set. Dissolving mental and emotional blocks will work to free you from financial fear and bring you closer to financial freedom. Second, you have to get clear on your financial goals. Over time, smart planning and realistic budgets can result in great rewards. Third, you have to have an action plan. Once your financial intentions match with your actions, you will be on the road to real wealth. Use these crystals to set yourself up for wealth.

AVENTURINE sets you up for a lucky break. This stone makes sure that you are in the right place at the right time, and then it's up to you to seize the opportunity. New job prospects? New tasks at work? Aventurine teaches you to say "yes" to everything that has the potential to bring you wealth.

CITRINE puts a stop to any negative money mind-chatter related to saving. Doubting yourself and your ability to save money is almost always an excuse to spend more money you don't have or shouldn't be spending. This crystal can bring a little sunshine to your budget and inspires you to approach saving with a positive attitude. Through working with Citrine, you might even discover that saving money is empowering and fun.

GARNET brings passion into your money. It draws attention to what makes you happy and how that can bring more abundance to your finances. Garnet also strengthens your foundation for your financial life.

IOLITE helps you break free of debt. If you have long-term debt to pay back or you consistently spend more than you have, Iolite teaches you to make mindful decisions so you can pull yourself out of debt and bring yourself closer to being wealthy.

JADE allows you to build your prosperity. It guides you to envision how you can be prosperous in all areas of your life.

MALACHITE transforms your money mind-set. If you have negative thought patterns or destructive long-held beliefs when it comes to money, this stone helps you change that. Do you believe it's hard to make money or that you aren't good with money? Do you think that wanting money makes you greedy? Malachite empowers you to move toward your financial targets without fear, doubt, stress, anxiety, worry, or any other toxic emotions that surround money and finances.

PYRITE attracts wealth. Working with this stone opens you up to new ways to acquire money, like new career ventures, gifts, and increased earnings. With Pyrite by your side, more money will come your way, but it might not be from where you expect.

TIGER'S EYE increases your motivation to create wealth and abundance. It keeps you focused and steady, and pushes you to work hard and stay dedicated to bringing your financial goals to life.

# CHANGING YOUR MONEY MIND-SET

### CRYSTAL INTENTION

## Money comes to me easily and effortlessly.

### CRYSTAL PRACTICE

1 Hold your crystals in both hands and state out loud, "Money comes to me easily and effortlessly."

2 Holding your Iolite in your hands, ask yourself, *How do I self-sabotage my money? How am I not showing up to my financial life? What are my limiting beliefs when it comes to money?* Use this time to reflect on these 3 questions, being completely honest with yourself.

3 Hold your Pyrite and look at it. Ask yourself, *If I were to change those behaviors and move toward success, what could I do today to take action?* Use this time to reflect on this question.

4 When you are finished, place your stones in your wallet, pocket, or purse. Every time you go to pay for something, see your crystals and be reminded of your intention.

# CREATING FINANCIAL SECURITY

JADE

GARNET

### CRYSTAL INTENTION

## I am financially secure.

### CRYSTAL PRACTICE

1 Hold your crystals in both hands and state your intention out loud, "I am financially secure."

2 Create a wealth bowl. Place an empty bowl in a prominent place in your living room or kitchen. Throw all your loose change, bills, coins from travels to different countries, and anything else that represents money to you into it.

3 Place your Jade and Garnet crystals in your bowl.

4 Continue to add to your bowl every week.

## For added prosperity:

*Wear a Jade necklace or a Jade bracelet on your left wrist to open up the energy of receiving.*

# ATTRACTING
# WEALTH

AVENTURINE

CITRINE

MALACHITE

PYRITE

TIGER'S EYE

**CRYSTAL INTENTION**

## I am wealthy.

**CRYSTAL PRACTICE**

1   Hold your crystals in both
    hands and state your intention
    out loud:
    "I am wealthy," 8 times.

2   Place Pyrite on top of your
    business card or desk.

3   Carry Citrine in your wallet or
    pocket.

4   Carry Malachite in your pocket
    for all business meetings.

5   Write down your financial goals
    on a piece of paper and place
    Tiger's Eye and Aventurine on
    top of the paper.

6   Leave all your crystals in place
    for 40 days.

7   After the 40 days, cleanse
    your crystals to be ready to
    use again for the next time
    you need to supercharge your
    wealth intention.

# crystal FAQs

**Q** I'VE HAD MY CRYSTAL FOR TWO DAYS. WHY ISN'T IT WORKING?

**A** *Does a diet work in two days? Does a fitness regimen work in two days?* Like any new program, it takes time and consistency to see the transformation. Working with crystals is no different. The magic is not the crystal; it's you. It's a tool to help you achieve your goal at a faster rate.

**Q** I HAVE MY CRYSTAL. NOW WHAT DO I DO?

**A** Spend some time with it. Put it to action! Use it in your daily life. If your intention for the crystal is to make money, have it around money. Put it in your wallet. Drop it into your coin jar. Place it on top of a business proposal.

If your intention for the crystal is love, keep it in the bedroom, perhaps on your nightstand. Place it over your heart for a moment before you go to sleep. Keep duos of crystals around to represent a partnership.

If your intention is to let go of stress, carry your crystal as a touchstone. When you start feeling stressed, grab on to your crystal and remind yourself to stop, breathe, let go. Touching the stone will help you to reaffirm your intention.

**Q** ARE WE TAKING TOO MANY CRYSTALS FROM THE EARTH WHEN WE USE THEM?

**A** The 52 crystals in this book are all plentiful and common stones. These are being mined horizontally, meaning limited intrusion on the Earth. It's not just how the crystals are mined—the bigger question is, how are miners being treated? It is very important to make sure the miners are being paid fair wages, have health support, and are being treated well. Strive to get your crystals from ethical sources.

**Q** ARE ALL CRYSTALS EXPENSIVE?

**A** No. Many people find that a tumbled stone is a great entryway into the crystal world. Tumbled stones are generally smaller than the palm of your hand and usually very affordable.

**Q** HOW DO I STORE MY CRYSTALS?

**A** When you're not using your crystals, you can put them in a bowl together, put them on your windowsill, or place them in a bag or pouch or anywhere else where they can enhance your space.

**Q** CAN I WORK WITH MORE THAN ONE CRYSTAL AT A TIME?

**A** When you are new to the crystal world, the best results come from working with one crystal at a time and focusing on one intention at a time. The first step to choosing where to start is to decide which intention you're going to focus on and which crystal will help you. Start with that one crystal first. Once you've transformed that area of your life, choose a new intention and new crystal.

You may choose to focus on one crystal/intention at a time, or you may find that you can balance several crystals/intentions at a time. Learn your own unique style of working with crystals and follow that, as long as you approach your intentions with the same level of commitment, whether you are working with one or five.

You may find that you need to work with some crystals longer than others. Certain areas may require more time and focus. The time frame will be different for everyone and every intention, so it's important to customize your crystal practice to what works for you.

**Q** WHAT ARE FIVE SIMPLE WAYS TO USE MY CRYSTAL?

**A** Carry it in your pocket or purse.
Wear it.
Place it on your nightstand.
Lay it on your body.
Meditate while holding it.

**Q** ARE CRYSTALS PART OF A RELIGION?

**A** Crystals are a tool to help you transform your life. Crystals are not part of and do not interfere with your religious practice; many clients have found that using crystals strengthened their practice. Crystals are an energy source, but they are not *the Source.*

**Q** HOW OFTEN DO I CLEANSE MY CRYSTAL?

**A** Crystals work best when they are cleansed because over time they absorb and accumulate energy from the environment around them and the people who touch them. It's always a good idea to cleanse your crystals when you first get them to ensure they are a clear slate for your intention.

As a general guideline, it is recommended that you cleanse your crystal every time you set a new intention, or at least once every 30 days.

# index

# acknowledgments

## muse /myo͞oz/
noun. a guiding spirit or source of inspiration

To all the muses who advised, inspired and believed in me when
no one else did. I would not have stayed on this journey without you.
Your love and support never go unnoticed.

MOTHER EARTH + HER CRYSTALS

TIMMI JANDRO

REID TRACY, PATTY GIFT + LISA CHENG AND HAY HOUSE TEAM

JENNIFER GOOCH HUMMER

SARA CARTER

SARAH BRATMAN

JESSICA CARREIRO

THE ENERGY MUSE TEAM

JASON, ORION, SOFIA ROSE, DEE, AND DAN

BETSY MCLAUGHLIN

MIKE STADVEC

JORDAN, MIKE, MICHAEL, LINDSEY, JOSH, ERIK, MATT, KATI, AND THE GP TEAM

HAN PARK

THE ENERGY MUSE COMMUNITY

# about the author

**Heather Askinosie** is a leading influencer on the power of crystals, feng shui, and holistic healing. For over 25 years, she has had the privilege of studying with the best healers from all over the world, who have passed down ancient teachings on how to utilize energy technology. In 2000, Heather co-founded Energy Muse with business partner Timmi Jandro. Energy Muse is a conscious lifestyle brand, providing tools of empowerment, inspiration, and hope in the tangible form of jewelry and crystals. Together, Heather and Timmi are helping people reconnect with the energy of the Earth to align with their highest self, realize their true calling, and tap into their own personal magnificence. You can visit them online at www.energymuse.com.

## Hello Crystal Lover,

Now that you've finished reading *CRYSTAL365*, it's time to put these crystal practices into action! To help you incorporate crystals further in your everyday life, I've created some special bonus resources for you to take your results to the next level. You can access them for free at: **www.energymuse.com/crystal365-bonus**. These resources are here to answer any burning crystal questions you have and will teach you even more about how to use crystals for the best results.

I can't wait to continue this crystal journey with you!

In gratitude,

Heather Askinosie

We hope you enjoyed this Hay House book. If you'd like to receive our online catalog featuring additional information on Hay House books and products, or if you'd like to find out more about the Hay Foundation, please contact:

Hay House, Inc., P.O. Box 5100, Carlsbad, CA 92018-5100
(760) 431-7695 or (800) 654-5126
(760) 431-6948 (fax) or (800) 650-5115 (fax)
www.hayhouse.com® • www.hayfoundation.org

———

*Published in Australia by:* Hay House Australia Pty. Ltd.,
18/36 Ralph St., Alexandria NSW 2015
*Phone:* 612-9669-4299 • *Fax:* 612-9669-4144
www.hayhouse.com.au

*Published in the United Kingdom by:* Hay House UK, Ltd.,
The Sixth Floor, Watson House, 54 Baker Street, London W1U 7BU
*Phone:* +44 (0)20 3927 7290 • *Fax:* +44 (0)20 3927 7291
www.hayhouse.co.uk

*Published in India by:* Hay House Publishers India,
Muskaan Complex, Plot No. 3, B-2, Vasant Kunj, New Delhi 110 070
*Phone:* 91-11-4176-1620 • *Fax:* 91-11-4176-1630
www.hayhouse.co.in

———

Access New Knowledge.
Anytime. Anywhere.

Learn and evolve at your own pace
with the world's leading experts.

www.hayhouseU.com

**Heather Askinosie** is a leading influencer on the power of crystals, Feng Shui, and holistic healing and the co-author of *Crystal Muse*. For over 25 years, she has had the privilege of studying with the best healers from all over the world, who have passed down ancient teachings on how to utilize energy technology. Heather is a co-founder of Energy Muse with business partner Timmi Jandro. Energy Muse is a crystal lifestyle company, providing tools of empowerment, inspiration, and hope in the form of jewelry and crystals. Together, Heather and Timmi are helping people reconnect with the energy of the Earth to align with their highest self, realize their true calling, and tap into their own personal magnificence. You can visit them online at www.energymuse.com.

HAY
HOUSE

Hay House USA
P.O. Box 5100, Carlsbad, CA 92018-5100
(760) 431-7695 or (800) 654-5126
(760) 431-6948 (fax) or (800) 650-5115 (fax)
www.hayhouse.com®
Tune in to HayHouseRadio.com®
for the best in inspirational talk radio featuring top Hay House authors!

Front cover design: Karla Baker
Front-cover photo: Sara Carter

Printed in the United States of America